The Great Columbus

F 8/3   3

The Great Columbus Experiment of 1908

WATERWORKS THAT CHANGED THE WORLD

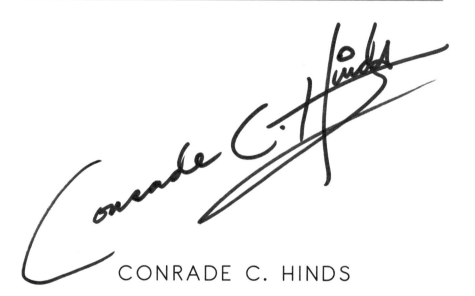

CONRADE C. HINDS

Charleston · London

THE
History
PRESS

Published by The History Press
Charleston, SC 29403
www.historypress.net

First published 2012

Manufactured in the United States

ISBN 978.1.60949.779.8

Library of Congress CIP data applied for.

Contents

CONTENTS

Preface

The history of the 1908 Columbus Experiment is a story about a community's quest for clean drinking water. Yet, most Americans, and in my experience, the people of Central Ohio, don't have an intrinsic understanding of their history because the earned wisdom and lessons embedded in the past are often not communicated or understood. Consequently, they are hardly ever exposed to what I call a premier historian.

A premier historian is not a doctoral candidate conducting research to establish tenure. Rather, this individual is a curious storyteller who can set the mood and reestablish the feeling of a particular place in time, recall the drive and the host of emotions and excitement that connect us to past events. Without the acute storyteller, the general public will likely not be able to fully appreciate or care to recall its own significant history. Many think that true history is only a chronological record of significant events that impacted a nation, institution or individual. This chronology may or may not include an explanation of the reasons behind the events recorded; most often, it is merely a list of mundane historical facts and moments devoid of analysis or holistic interpretation of the world surrounding the events.

Significant events will also not be recalled as great history because they lack the polish of the storyteller's narration. This is why so many stories that are not quite as sophisticated in content or meaningful get ample attention when presented with spoken commentary or explanation in a movie or television series. The viewer is given information while being able to observe and imaginatively place themselves safely in the actions.

Although history is a story of the past, I have found that people will appreciate and relate to history more when they can connect with people from that era who have made even a small impression on them. For instance, fans of westerns may recognize 1907 as the year John Wayne made his screen debut. Likewise, 1908 saw the birth of Mel Blanc, the man who was the voice of so many cartoon characters, such as Bugs Bunny and Daffy Duck, that so many grew up watching. Those who had an influence on an era are then remembered as shaping the twentieth century and our lives. So in order to bring to life the events and culture surrounding the 1908 Columbus Experiment, I have cited a number of peripheral and mainstream headlines from the period as well as people who were affected by the results of Columbus' aggressive implementation of a new kind of public service.

The history of the 1908 Columbus Experiment and its impact on public health standards affects everyone worldwide. Many people die each day because they lack access to clean, potable water. The World Health Organization (WHO) estimates that thirteen thousand children die each day due to water-borne diseases. The Columbus Experiment itself was the amalgamation of America's best technology and engineering work, the progress garnered from nineteenth-century public health innovators and the harsh lessons learned from the minimal sanitary standards in medical treatment during the Civil War. It is imperative to recognize that the true measure of the relevance of local homespun history is the impact that it has on the world. After all, the world has always played a large role in determining many of the daily activities associated with life in rural, small town and urban America. Progress in the developing nations in both hemispheres in the early twentieth century was unmistakably contagious and knew few boundaries.

Acknowledgements

O hio wasn't built by America, but it is my opinion that America was built by Ohio's broad application of its profound innovative spirit, and for that, I am very grateful.

Thank you, Tom Betti and Doreen Uhas Sauer, for extending an invitation to participate in writing a book for the Columbus Landmarks Foundation's history book series, and to my wife, Dr. Janet L. Hinds, for her help in scholarly research and generous sharing. Thanks to the Education Committee of the Columbus Landmarks Foundation for their insight and creativity. A note of gratitude to the following: Dr. Joseph and Ruth Waggener; Dr. Richard and Gloria Clossman; Charles Sappenfield; Arthur and Beverly Brown; George W. Cox; David and Ann Dale; Marvin and Elsa Reichle; and Martin and Helen Schwartz. Thank you all for your positive encouragement and for opening the doors of opportunity for me over the past forty-plus years. And my continued thanks to all of those who supported preserving Columbus' heritage as an international leader in the field of water and wastewater technology: John Doutt, Jeff Hubbard, Lynn Kelly, Tom Galitza, Tom Camden, Dr. Rick Westerfield, Craig Charleston, Anthony Kohler, Debbie Ashley, Bill Clark, Lee White, Steve Tiberi, Dan Davis, John Wenig, Jay Gillispie, and the staff of The Dublin Road Water Plant past and present.

A special thanks to my late parents and grandparents, Dr. Conrade and Ada Hinds and Russell and Ethel Davidson for sharing their insight and wisdom. I would also like to extend my gratitude to John and Ellen Stukenberg, Chuck Rinehart, Dave Busch and Dean Bortz for their confidence in me as an educator. Thanks also to John Sauer, for his constructive editing, and to the Board of Columbus Landmarks Foundation, for their support and the ever-creative Education Committee. And finally, to Joe Gartrell of The History Press.

Photo credits: Columbus Metropolitan Library Image Collections (CML), Ferdinand Hamburger Archives at The John Hopkins University (FHJH), the Columbus Dispatch (CD), Columbus Citizen Journal (CCJ), Conrade Hinds Collection (CH), Private Collection (PC), Ohio Historic Society, Columbus Division of Water (CDW) and the Library of Congress.

Introduction

Too many pivotal events in America often go unappreciated by the general public because people are disconnected by generations and believe that they do not possess any tangible connection to past events. The 1908 Columbus Experiment was like the 1969 moon landing to the world's engineering and emerging public health community of that time. The massive potable public waterworks project provided a public health service that the people of Columbus and Central Ohio eventually began to take for granted. A negative connotation that is widely used in many realms of modern society is that once something or someone has finished or completed a task, it soon becomes a part of history and is generally ignored. In other words, it becomes yesterday's news, and news is only good if it is served fresh daily. Also, as many of these great accomplishments begin to be taken for granted, the memories, records and history of the work, as well as the sacrifice involved in securing various advancements, are soon labeled as antiquated and are erased and forgotten. An unfortunate example of this was the tragic loss of the construction drawings, details and artifacts of the former West Side Pumping Station on Old Dublin Avenue and the original East Side station on Nelson Road.

In the late 1970s, these precious items were not loaned but given to the developer or owner of the Waterworks Restaurant, whose office was located at 225 North Front Street, for display and to highlight the establishment's motif. After all, the West Side Pumping Station stopped operation in 1908 and was completely demolished shortly after World War II to make way

Scioto River Pumping Station employees pose for a photo on the various decks of the Holly Triple Expansion Steam Engine. The actual pumps are pictured on the lower level. *CDW.*

for an expansion of the city's electric power generating plant. The old East Side Pumping Station was razed shortly afterward. It is quite evident that no one in the city's administration saw any value in these documents. When the restaurant closed in 1987, all of these items were sold at public auction to individuals. These items had been city property and part of Columbus' heritage and should not have been given away or sold.

Clearly, the actions of people and events over the years still have a great impact on the manner in which we live, work, hope and play today. Columbus is the capital of a great state that recognized no boundaries when it came to fostering the sons and daughters of the Industrial Revolution. Its attitude regarding advancement was echoed decades later by the American industrialist Henry J. Kaiser, who said, "Find a need and fill it" and "Problems are opportunities in work clothes." Kaiser's own homegrown slogans were designed to inspire hard work and foster a sense of common goals within a working community. Ohioans demonstrated an understanding of a common goal early on with the construction of the canal system, which fostered commerce and trade throughout the region. It is interesting to note that Kaiser's early career is dominated by the construction of large public works projects, such as water-supply dams, roads and bridges.

The story of the Great Columbus Experiment of 1908 may be a forgotten triumph to most people. But it was the catalyst that helped set a precedent for delivering clean and uncontaminated drinking water on a large scale, not only to the city of Columbus but also to America and the world. No longer would water utilities render marginal quality water for a few consumers and high pressure for just fighting fires. (Developing countries of the twentieth century were still plagued by devastating town fires as well as disease epidemics.) The 1908 Experiment involved a series of intriguing events, stalled and resurrected plans and deaths, which ranged from the ordinary to the notable.

As with all inventions and new methods, the Columbus Experiment is linked to a number of large and small connections that occurred in the nineteenth century's industrial age and the beginning years of the Progressive movement. The local Columbus newspapers, of course, featured stories of the political maneuvering over the need for a new water storage dam and treatment works. But they also told the Columbus community the events occurring throughout the world. These seemingly remote events would, in time, have an effect on the front door of everyone's life in Columbus. But the Columbus Experiment would also have a reciprocating and long lasting effect on the general standard of living for people throughout the world.

CHAPTER ONE
Waterborne Diseases, Pioneers and Connections

To fully appreciate the vast impact of the Columbus Experiment, we must take a brief look at the individuals whose lives and actions served as the priming agent in steering the events associated with the experiment. By the 1900s, the average life expectancy for Americans was forty-seven years. That figure includes the mortality rate among children under the age of two who often succumbed to waterborne disease because of an undeveloped immune system and a wide array of foreign pathogens.

The first water facility to deliver water to an entire town was built in Paisley, Scotland, in 1804 and was constructed by John Gibb. Within three years, filtered water was being piped directly to customers in Glasgow, Scotland. In 1806, a large water treatment plant began operating in Paris. The plant's filters were made of sand and charcoal and were renewed every six hours. Pumps were driven by actual horses working in three shifts. Water was settled for twelve hours before filtration.

The latter part of the nineteenth century was a time when only men had the right to vote, which also meant they had the right to approve funding levies for large capital infrastructure improvement projects such as water and wastewater utilities. This era was the beginning of western culture gaining an understanding of the nature of bacterial infections as they related to a person's general hygiene habits. Often, a single death would bring only sorrow from an immediate or extended family. But when multiple deaths resulted from similar symptoms, communities began to take notice. For centuries, infamous plagues have taken their toll on the world's population.

And in the end, it was accepted as a divine intervention as a result of the world's sinful nature. In time, instead of bowing to the superstitions that blamed and focused only on individuals' sinful proclivities, pioneering medical practitioners began to question the world's ignorance of nature itself and started a quest to unlock the real cause of disease.

Typhoid had plagued the general population for centuries. Adding to that, a cholera epidemic struck America in 1831 and again in 1832 and was thought to have begun originally in the Far East or India. This cholera epidemic made its way around the world many times through the end of the century, killing large numbers of common innocent people. It caused profuse and violent cramps, vomiting and diarrhea and dehydration so severe that the blood thickened and the skin became deathlike and blue. Under these conditions, cholera victims can die in a matter of hours. The nineteenth century brought many transformations in industrial, urban, political and cultural life that were intimately connected with discussions about the need to promote proper public health practices and the reason and causes of these diseases. Attempts to explain epidemics such as cholera and typhoid involved every part of society.

For most of the nineteenth century, scientists, physicians and sophisticated lay people generally believed cholera was not contagious. This was based on doctors having contact with cholera patients without falling ill. This was an accurate observation since cholera is usually transmitted through contaminated drinking water, as British physician Dr. John Snow (1813–1858) demonstrated in 1855.

Snow began investigating the cause of cholera epidemics by mapping a number of cholera outbreaks that occurred in London in 1849. During these outbreaks, a sizable number of the death victims had been obtaining what they presumed to be potable water from two water-pumping companies that used the Thames River as their source of supply. The location of these pumping stations was in the worst place possible for healthy consumption and the best place for promoting epidemics of diseases such as cholera and typhoid. In this case, it was just downstream from a sewage-effluent outlet. As certain, almost divine luck would have it, one of the supply station companies changed its water source intake conduit to an area along the Thames that was far less polluted, which resulted in significantly fewer deaths among consumers.

Snow began plotting the distribution of death occurrences throughout London on a special map and was able to deduce that a significantly high number of deaths occurred near a water-pump stand located at Broad Street in London. As a result of Snow's carefully documented data, he was able to convince the local authorities to take the pump out of public service. The number of cholera deaths was substantially reduced almost instantly.

Snow's work stands out as one of the world's most famous and earliest cases of geography and maps being utilized to gain an understanding about how diseases are spread in general populations. His identification of the Broad Street pump as the cause of the epidemic is considered the classic example of epidemiology. Today, specially trained medical geographers and medical practitioners routinely use mapping and advanced technology to understand the diffusion and spread of diseases.

Another influence in the Columbus Experiment is Hungarian physician and obstetrician Ignaz Semmelweis (1818–1865), also a medical pioneer, who, in 1847, reduced infant mortality at a hospital in Vienna after realizing that an extremely high occurrence of death from puerperal fever resulted from women who were attended by male physicians. Often, many of these doctors had earlier that same day conducted an autopsy. It should be noted that midwife deliveries were regarded in the nineteenth century as being relatively safe. Semmelweis insisted doctors wash and disinfect their hands with chlorinated lime water prior to examining expectant mothers. By using this protocol, the mortality rate from childbirth was reduced from 18.0 to 2.2 percent at Semmelweis' hospital.

In light of this success, Semmelweis' methods and theories were viciously attacked by the Viennese medical leadership and community. Virtually everyone rejected his basic and groundbreaking theoretical innovation that stated a disease had only one cause—the lack of cleanliness. Although Semmelweis published his findings in 1850, his work was not appreciated by his medical peers and consequently resulted in the discontinued use of his disinfection protocols and procedures. But Semmelweis' work and methods did gain widespread acceptance some years following his death.

The use of general disinfection practices became widely accepted after the British surgeon Joseph Lister (1827–1912) introduced and began using antiseptics in 1865. In the 1870s, Lister worked to promote and introduce practical sterile methods of surgery based on the germ theory of disease. Lister's contributions were generally seen as a result of the research and findings of the French chemist Louis Pasteur (1822–1895). Pasteur's research produced findings that supported the "germ theory of disease" that had been proposed by Italian entomologist Agostino Bassi (1773–1856) decades earlier. His work proved that there is more to exploring than just sailing to places unknown. Bassi's baton was passed to Pasteur, who was a front-runner in proving the practical merits of the germ theory and development of bacteriology as a viable science. Simply stated, the germ theory purported that microorganisms were the cause and foundation of many diseases. After decades of controversy, the germ theory was validated in the late nineteenth century and is now a fundamental part of modern medicine and clinical microbiology, leading to such important innovations as antibiotics and hygienic practices.

Along with Pasteur, pioneer and German physician Heinrich Robert Koch (1843–1910) used the germ theory in isolating the tuberculosis organism (1882) and *Vibrio cholerae* (1883), the bacterium that causes cholera. Koch was the first scientist to devise a series of tests used to assess the germ theory of disease. In 1885, he became professor of hygiene at the University of Berlin, and in 1891, he was appointed to be director of the Prussian Institute for Infectious Diseases. It is interesting to note that Koch's students identified the organisms responsible for tetanus, bubonic plague, diphtheria, pneumonia, gonorrhea, cerebrospinal meningitis, syphilis and leprosy by using his procedures and research methodology. Pasteur and Koch are regarded as the founders of microbiology and bacteriology. After decades of controversy, the germ theory was validated in the late nineteenth century. It is now a fundamental part of modern medicine and clinical microbiology, having paved the way for twentieth-century antibiotics, hygienic practices and the justification for public works such as the Columbus Experiment.

In 1880, the German pathologist and bacteriologist Karl Joseph Eberth (1835–1926) described an organism that he suspected was the cause of typhus. While in 1884, another German pathologist, Georg Theodor August Gaffky (1850–1918), confirmed Eberth's findings, and the organism was called the Gaffky-Eberth bacillus. Today, this organism is known in scientific terms as *Salmonella typhi* and is the cause of the dreaded typhoid fever. It is interesting to note that Gaffky worked as an assistant to Heinrich Robert Koch, and it was under Koch's leadership that Gaffky and several associates developed a number of bacteriological research protocols. This work was instrumental in advancing the success in identifying and recognizing the causes of a wide variety of infectious diseases.

As in the nineteenth century, most Americans today still do not fully comprehend the true nature of disease epidemics. So in order to have a full appreciation of the social and public health challenges as well as the hardships of waterborne disease inflected on a population, it is best to examine the three most common waterborne diseases, starting with typhoid.

An illustration of how typhoid bacteria could easily contaminate a water well. *Library of Congress.*

Typhoid fever is a bacterial disease that is transmitted by the ingestion of food or water contaminated with the feces of an infected person. The offending bacterium is *Salmonella typhi*. Once ingested, the bacteria then passes through the intestinal wall and grows best at 98.6 degrees Fahrenheit, the average body temperature for humans. It affects populations worldwide even today. The infection has received a variety of names over the years, including gastric fever, abdominal typhus, infantile remittent fever, slow fever, nervous fever and pathogenic fever. Modern sanitation technology and hygienic practices, such as water and wastewater treatment, has reduced the disease's impact significantly in the last century and a half.

The course of untreated typhoid fever is divided into four individual stages, each lasting approximately one week. In the first week, there is a slowly rising temperature with relative malaise, headache and cough. A bloody nose is seen in a quarter of cases, and abdominal pain is also possible. In the second week of the infection, the patient lies prostrate and suffers from high fever, about 104 degrees. Delirium is frequent, often calm, but it can sometimes spike. From this delirium, typhoid earns the nickname of "nervous fever." Rose spots appear on the lower chest and abdomen in around a third of patients. The abdomen is distended and painful in the right lower quadrant where intestinal rumbling, known as borborygmi, can be heard. Diarrhea can occur in this stage; constipation is also frequent. The major symptom of this fever is that the fever usually rises in the afternoon up to the first and second week.

In the third week of typhoid fever, a number of complications can occur, such as an intestinal hemorrhage caused by bleeding in congested lymphoid nodules. This can be very serious but is usually not fatal. Intestinal perforation in the small intestine is a very serious complication and is frequently fatal. This can happen without any alarming symptoms until septicemia or diffuse peritonitis sets in. Encephalitis, which is an inflammation of the brain, results in neuropsychiatric symptoms, also known as "muttering delirium" or "coma vigil," with picking at bedclothes or imaginary objects.

The fever is still very high and oscillates very little over twenty-four hours. Dehydration ensues, and the patient is thoroughly delirious in what is called a typhoid state. By the end of the third week, the fever has started, reducing and returning to normal. This carries on into the fourth and final week when all other symptoms subside. Obviously, the key to surviving typhoid fever is to have and maintain an efficient immune system.

The transmission of the bacteria that causes typhoid fever usually occurs through maintaining poor hygiene habits and public sanitation conditions. It is sometimes also caused by flying insects that have previously fed on feces. Public education campaigns encouraging people to wash their hands after defecating and before handling food are an important component in controlling the spread of this disease as much today as in the past. According to statistics from the United States Centers for Disease Control and Prevention (CDC), the chlorination of drinking water has led to dramatic decreases in the transmission of typhoid fever in the U.S.

A person may become an asymptomatic carrier of typhoid fever. That means that they are suffering no symptoms but are very capable of infecting others. As mentioned previously, sanitation and hygiene are the critical measures that can be taken to prevent typhoid. Typhoid does not affect animals, so it is only transmitted from human to human. Typhoid can only spread in environments where human feces or urine is able to come into contact with food or drinking water.

Next on our list of classic waterborne diseases is cholera. The transmission of cholera occurs primarily by drinking water or eating food that has been contaminated by the fecal matter from an infected individual, and this may include someone who displays no symptoms. It is also transmitted when people consume fecal-contaminated food and water. This is often the result of substandard sanitary practices at home and in public eating establishments, where fortunately signs are now being posted to remind workers and the public about the importance of simply washing hands following routine body waste elimination.

Cholera is an infection generally concentrated in the small intestine and is caused by bacteria called *Vibrio cholerae*. The most common symptoms are severe diarrhea and vomiting that result in rapid dehydration followed by an imbalance in electrolytes. This condition frequently results in death. It is imperative that the ill person quickly receive an oral rehydration solution to replace the body's water and essential electrolytes. In the nineteenth century, due to the lack of medical treatment with intravenous fluids and antibiotics that were not widely used or even available until the 1930s, infected individuals did not improve quickly, and the disease would continue to advance to a dangerous level. As mentioned earlier, cholera was one of the earliest infectious diseases to be studied using epidemiological protocols and methods. Still, even in the twenty-first century, approximately 3,000,000 to 5,000,000 people are affected worldwide each year, and between 100,000 and 130,000 people die on average annually as a result.

Although cholera may be life threatening, prevention of this disease, like typhoid, is normally straightforward if proper sanitation practices are implemented. In developed countries, due to nearly universal advanced water treatment and sanitation practices, cholera is no longer a major health threat. The last major outbreak of cholera in the United States occurred around the time the Columbus Experiment was being implemented. Effective sanitation practices, if instituted and adhered to in time, are usually sufficient to stop an epidemic. There are several points along the cholera transmission path where the disease can be curtailed.

First, proper disposal and treatment of infected fecal wastewater produced by cholera victims and all contaminated materials, including items such as clothing and bedding, is essential. All materials that come in contact with cholera patients should be sanitized by washing in hot water, using chlorine bleach if possible to disinfect the contaminated items. Hands that touch cholera patients or their clothing, bedding and so on should also be thoroughly cleaned and disinfected with chlorinated water or other effective antimicrobial agents.

Second, antibacterial treatment of general sewage by chlorine or other effective treatment before it is reintroduced into the natural waterways or underground water supplies helps prevent undiagnosed patients from inadvertently spreading the disease. In regards to water purification, all water used for drinking, washing or cooking should be sterilized by boiling, chlorination, water treatment or antimicrobial filtration in any area where cholera may be present. Chlorinating and boiling water are by far the least expensive (and have been proven to be the most effective) means of halting cholera transmission. Boiling water is heated hot enough and long enough to kill microorganisms that normally live in water at room temperature. Those who live near sea level should bring water to a vigorous rolling boil for at least one minute; three minutes is recommended for altitudes higher than five thousand feet. Boiling does not leave a residual disinfectant in the water, so water that is boiled and then stored for any length of time may acquire new pathogens.

In any case, public health education and adherence to appropriate sanitation practices are of primary importance to help prevent and control transmission of cholera and other diseases. Warnings about possible cholera contamination should be posted around contaminated water sources with directions on how to decontaminate the water for possible use. This was difficult in the early years because surveillance practices were not fully developed or comprehensive. Surveillance and prompt reporting allow for containing cholera epidemics rapidly. Cholera exists as a seasonal disease in many endemic countries, occurring annually mostly during rainy seasons. Surveillance systems can provide early alerts to outbreaks and lead to a coordinated response and preparedness plans. Efficient surveillance systems can also improve the risk assessment for potential cholera outbreaks. Understanding the seasonality and location of outbreaks provides guidance for improving cholera control activities for the most vulnerable.

Endemic, epidemic and pandemic are three terms referring to the spread of infectious diseases among a population on different scales. An infection is endemic when it constantly affects a specific and limited group of people and at a stable rate. An epidemic occurs when new cases of a certain disease in a given human population during a given period substantially exceed the normal rate of occurrences. But unlike an epidemic, a pandemic affects an extremely large number of people and a much larger geographical region.

A severe cholera pandemic that lasted from 1827 to 1835 hit the United States and Europe. Although cholera started out as a local disease, it became one of the most widespread and deadly diseases of the nineteenth century, killing millions of people. In Russia alone, between 1847 and 1851, more than one million people perished from the disease. An estimated fifty thousand Americans died during the second pandemic. It is not widely known that between 1900 and 1920, approximately eight million people died of cholera in India while it was under British colonial rule.

Waterborne Diseases, Pioneers and Connections

Cholera became the first disease that was widely reported on in the United States due to the significant effects it had on health. John Snow, in 1854, was the first to identify the importance of contaminated water in its cause. Cholera is now no longer considered a pressing health threat in Europe and North America due to filtering and chlorination of water supplies, but it still heavily affects populations in developing countries.

In the past, people traveling in ships would hoist a yellow quarantine flag if one or more of the crew members suffered from cholera. Passengers from boats with a yellow flag displayed would not be allowed to disembark at any harbor for an extended period, typically thirty to forty days.

Dysentery is an inflammatory disorder of the intestine, especially of the colon, that results in severe diarrhea containing mucus, blood or both in the feces, as well as fever, abdominal pain and rectal tenesmus. It was formerly known as flux, or the "bloody flux disease," and if a person remains untreated, dysentery can be fatal. Dysentery results from viral, bacterial or protozoan infections or parasitic infestations. These pathogens typically reach the large intestine after contaminated food or water is orally ingested or through oral contact with contaminated objects, such as hands.

In order to prevent and reduce the risk of contracting dysentery, the following precautions are suggested. Hands should be washed following body waste elimination or after contact with an infected person and regularly throughout the day. In addition, hands should be washed prior to handling, cooking and eating food; handling babies; and feeding young or elderly individuals. Contact with someone known to have dysentery should be kept at a minimum, and clothes should be washed afterward using hot water and detergent. Sharing items such as towels and face cloths should also be avoided.

During the nineteenth century, more soldiers and sailors were estimated to have died from the bloody flux than in combat. Typhus and dysentery decimated Napoleon's grand army in Russia, and more than eighty thousand Union troops died of dysentery during the American Civil War.

CHAPTER TWO

Civil War

Disease Deaths

W hile the average soldier believed the bullet was his most nefarious foe, disease was the biggest killer of the war. Of the Federal dead, roughly three out of five men died of disease; for the Confederates, perhaps two out of three. One of the reasons for the high rates of disease was the slipshod recruiting process that allowed under- or over-age men and those in noticeably poor health to join the armies on both sides, especially in the first year of the war. In fact, by late 1862, some 200,000 recruits who had been accepted for service were judged physically unfit and discharged, either because they had fallen ill or because a routine examination revealed their frail condition.

About half of the deaths from disease during the Civil War were caused by intestinal disorders, mainly typhoid fever, diarrhea and dysentery. The remainder died from pneumonia and tuberculosis. Camps populated by young soldiers who had never before been exposed to a large variety of common contagious diseases were plagued by outbreaks of measles, chickenpox, mumps and whooping cough.

The culprit in most cases of wartime illness, however, was the shocking filth of the army camps themselves. An inspector in late 1861 found most Federal camps "littered with refuse, food and other rubbish, sometimes in an offensive state of decomposition; slops deposited in pits within the camp limits or thrown out of broadcast; heaps of manure and offal close to the camp." As a result, bacteria and viruses spread through camps like wildfire. Bowel disorders constituted the soldiers' most common complaint. The Union army reported that more than 995 out of every 1,000 men eventually

Clean drinking water was rarely available for Civil War soldiers, so it was common for soldiers who were off duty, such as the Union soldiers pictured here, to enjoy beer and spirits. *CML.*

contracted chronic diarrhea or dysentery during the war; the Confederates fared no better.

Typhoid fever was even more devastating. Perhaps one-fourth of noncombat deaths in the Confederacy resulted from this disease. At the same time, malaria spread through camps located next to stagnant swamps teeming with anopheles mosquito. Although treatment with quinine reduced fatalities, malaria nevertheless struck approximately one-fourth of all servicemen. The Union army alone reported one million cases of it during the course of the war. Poor diet and exposure to the elements only added to the burden. A simple cold often developed into pneumonia, which was the third leading killer disease of the war, after typhoid and dysentery.

At least 618,000 Americans died in the Civil War, and some experts say the toll reached 700,000. The number that is most often cited is 620,000. At any rate, these casualties exceed the nation's loss in all its other wars, from the Revolutionary War, which started in the 1770s, through the end of the Vietnam War in the 1970s.

Between 2,500,000 and 2,750,000 men comprised the Union army. The Union's losses, by the best estimates, were 110,070 battle deaths and 250,152 deaths from disease—totaling 360,222 dead. The Confederate strength, known less accurately because of missing records, had between 750,000 and 1,250,000 men. It is estimated that losses in battle deaths were around 94,000 and disease claimed about 164,000 for a total of 258,000 dead.

Throughout the war, both the South and the North struggled to improve the level of medical care given to their men. In many ways, their efforts assisted in the birth of modern medicine in the United States. More complete records on medical and surgical activities were kept during the war than ever before. Doctors became more adept at surgery and at the use of anesthesia, and perhaps most importantly, a greater understanding of the relationship between cleanliness, diet and disease was gained not only by the medical establishment but also by the public at large. Another important advancement took place in the field of nursing, where respect for the role of women in medicine rose considerably among both doctors and patients.

In June 1861, a private relief agency was created by federal legislation and was known as the United States Sanitary Commission. Its purpose was to support sick and wounded soldiers of the U.S. Army during the American Civil War. It operated across the North and enlisted thousands of volunteers. The volunteers collected donations, worked as nurses, supplied and ran kitchens in army camps, soldiers' homes and lodges for traveling or disabled soldiers. They also made uniforms and organized sanitary fairs to support the Union army with funds and supplies. The commission was directed by Frederick Law Olmsted, the famous landscape architect who designed New York's Central Park.

Another untold advancement in public health services and preventing epidemics was early practice of embalming. Modern embalming really got its start during the tragic years of the Civil War. Union physician Dr. Thomas Holmes received a commission as a captain in the Army Medical Corps and was assigned to Washington, D.C., where he embalmed many army officers killed in battle. Colonel Elmer E. Ellsworth was the first military casualty of the American Civil War. On May 24, 1861, along with his New York City Volunteer Regiment (which was made up mostly of New York City firemen), Colonel Ellsworth went to remove a large Confederate flag from the roof of the Marshall House Hotel in Alexandria, Virginia. It was there that he was shot in the chest with a shotgun blast and killed. Upon the return of his body to the Washington navy yard, Dr. Thomas Holmes visited President Lincoln and offered to embalm the body free of charge. He was subsequently given permission to do so. It is reported that Mrs. Lincoln was so impressed with Colonel Ellsworth's appearance she requested that the same embalmer prepare their son's body when he died. Willie Lincoln was embalmed in the Green Room in February 1862 before his funeral in the East Room. Dr. Holmes reportedly embalmed over four thousand soldiers and officers.

President Lincoln took a great interest in embalming and directed the Quartermaster Corps to utilize embalming to allow the return of Union dead to their home towns for proper burial. When he realized the commercial potential of embalming, Holmes resigned his commission and began offering embalming to the public for $100. But after the Civil War, embalming fell into disuse due to a lack of demand. Moreover, few knew how to do the procedure. The "undertakers" of the day limited their efforts to ice to ward off decomposition long enough to have a funeral.

The primary purpose of embalming is for disinfection and to prevent epidemics. While some pathogens die soon after the death of the host, it is also true that many dangerous organisms have the ability to survive for long periods of time in dead tissues. Persons coming in direct contact with the un-embalmed body can become infected, and there is also the possibility of flies or other agents transferring pathogens to humans and infecting them.

Abraham Lincoln was embalmed after his assassination in April 1865. In order to prevent anyone from stealing Lincoln's body, Lincoln's eldest son, Robert, called for Lincoln's exhumation in 1901 and his reburial in a concrete vault in the burial room of his tomb in Springfield, Illinois. His features were still intact and very recognizable, even thirty-six years after his death.

CHAPTER THREE

The Chicago Fire Era and Changing Nature

The Era of Midwestern Problem Solving

The start of the 1870s marked five years since the end of the Civil War and the death of Abraham Lincoln. Northern cities such as Columbus, Cleveland, Cincinnati and Chicago were experiencing substantial growth during the postwar reconstruction years. At the start of this new decade, the City of Columbus began taking steps to build and develop a public water supply and distribution system to provide for household needs; at the same time, the City worked toward developing a system for general fire protection. Under the leadership of Columbus' first water superintendent, Wesley Royce, the first waterworks consisted of a pump house, a well that was 20-feet in diameter and a 256-foot filter gallery built to treat the raw well water. The new "waterworks" was a brick masonry building that housed a steam-powered pumping station that pumped water directly to the city's main pipelines. During major fire emergencies, valves installed in the filter gallery prevented raw water from flowing directly in the distribution system in order to maintain what was known as "fire pressure."

In the autumn of 1871, the Columbus Water Works started pumping water to the booming post–Civil War city through the first pump station located at the confluence of the Olentangy River and Scioto River on Dublin Avenue. Columbus also began laying both water mains and sewer lines to service the community. A young man from Delaware, Ohio, named Jerry O'Shaughnessy started out as a laborer working on the construction of this first pump station and rose to the position of superintendent in 1896.

Columbus' first waterworks pumping station was placed in service in 1871 and supplied raw well water. *CDW.*

Until 1870, Columbus residents obtained their water from private wells, springs and cisterns. In the year after the Civil War ended, Columbus had approximately 1,700 water wells in the city with a population of 32,000. That same year saw the establishment of the Ohio Agricultural and Mechanical College (which later became the Ohio State University) at the strong urging of Governor Rutherford B. Hayes, and it was decided that a new college would be placed near the state legislature in Columbus. The college was founded as a land-grant university in accordance with the Morrill Act of 1862. The school was originally situated within a farming community located on the northern edge of Columbus and was intended to matriculate students of various agricultural and mechanical disciplines. Also, Ohio Northern University was founded in Ada, Ohio, the following year, in 1871, and it affiliated with the United Methodist Church. The university would turn out some of Ohio's finest infrastructure and county engineers.

With the rapid growth of Columbus, an upgraded pumping station with increased capacity was constructed in 1889, adjacent to the original facility. But there remained one significant problem in that the water pumped from these facilities was not safe for human consumption. This was due to the various small villages north of the city that discharged raw sewage into Alum Creek and the Olentangy River. The sewage discharged into the water supply was causing contamination that resulted in a number of typhoid epidemics in the late 1800s. Epidemics of typhoid and other waterborne diseases occurred as a result of people dumping sewage directly into the river and its tributaries.

Many tragic events occurred in the 1870s, and they became hard lessons in the nineteenth century as urban areas grew. Historians agree that the Chicago Fire that broke out on the evening of October 8, 1871, did indeed start in the barn of Mr. and Mrs. Patrick O'Leary. While the blaze ironically spared the O'Leary home, which was located on the west side of the city, much of the rest of Chicago was not so fortunate. The fire died out early Tuesday morning (October 10), but not before it had cut a swath more than three square miles long through Chicago. Property valued at $192 million was destroyed, 100,000 people were left homeless and 300 people lost their lives. The results of the fire showed Columbus that it was on the right track and very timely in establishing the public waterworks.

The late nineteenth century witnessed municipal administrations taking on bold public works projects that had never before been tried in an effort to ensure the public's health. Chicago set a standard on what limits a city would and could take to harness nature and redirect its energy to maintain a viable supply of drinking water. Sixty-five in every 100,000 people in Chicago were dying from typhoid fever as early sewage systems discharged waste directly into Lake Michigan or into the river that led to the lake.

In 1887, Rudolph Hering (1847–1923), one of the great pioneers of modern environmental technology, proposed a bold engineering feat, one that would redirect the water to the Mississippi River through the city's first artificial canal. Hering noted that the Great Lakes and the Mississippi were separated by an eight-foot ridge, located twelve miles west of the lake shore. Diseases stemming from water contaminated with human waste escalated in Chicago, creating a state of emergency during the second half of the nineteenth century. To reverse the flow of the Chicago River, Hering proposed cutting a twenty-eight-mile canal from the south

Rudolph Hering (1847–1923) helped implement many modern methods of sanitary engineering that were first developed by Ellen Swallow Richards and were involved in the Chicago River reversal project. He also worked with John Gregory on the Columbus Experiment. *PC.*

branch of the river through the low summit and down toward Lockport, Illinois. By 1900, engineers had succeeded in reversing the Chicago River's flow and preserving Lake Michigan's drinking water.

A project of this size was needed due to water contamination, as citizens were constantly plagued by typhoid fever, cholera and dysentery. In 1854, a cholera epidemic took the lives of 2 to 5 percent of America's population. Deaths from typhoid fever during the forty years between 1860 and 1900 averaged 65 individuals per 100,000 persons each year. The worst year was 1891, when the death rate from typhoid was 174 per 100,000 persons. This local disease epidemic resulting from water polluted by human waste brought about a serious state of emergency.

The alarming death rates that resulted from this condition presented the city administration with a grim water-supply problem and sparked the development of gigantic engineering initiatives that, like the Columbus Experiment, captured international attention. Construction was completed in 1869 on the present Chicago Avenue Pumping Station and the Chicago Water Tower, the only municipal building to survive the Great Chicago Fire undamaged. In 1871, an underground tunnel was constructed to deliver water from an intake crib located two miles from the shoreline in Lake Michigan, and the first major attempt was made to reverse the flow of the Chicago River. The flow in this canal, commonly known as the Sanitary and Ship Canal, or main channel, is controlled by locks at the mouth of the Chicago River and at Lockport. Thus, Chicago had built the first of its own rivers to dispose of wastewaters.

In 1910, another small artificial river was completed by building a dam, lock and pumping plant at Wilmette and by digging the North Shore channel, connecting Lake Michigan with the north branch of the Chicago River. The waste from the north suburban communities of Evanston, Wilmette, Winnetka and others were diverted away from the lake and drained through the newly created main canal. This artificial channel is eight miles long.

One of the suppliers of equipment to do the mass excavation was the Bucyrus Foundry and Manufacturing Company. In its early history, Bucyrus was an early producer of steam shovels, operating from its headquarters and manufacturing facility in Bucyrus, Ohio, beginning in 1880. In 1904, Bucyrus would also build and supply 77 of the 102 steam shovels used during the excavation of the Panama Canal.

Chicago demonstrated to the world that an American Midwestern city would not just sit complacently idle while its citizens suffered from disease. Columbus easily borrowed the gumption required to make the Columbus Experiment happen from its Midwest neighbor, Chicago.

CHAPTER FOUR

Famous Victims

Typhoid fever and most other waterborne disease by no means plagued only the poor and less fortunate in society. It was known to strike down the wealthy and powerful at anytime, and we will see later that one such individual, while at the top of the political ladder of influence, was struck down by typhoid fever, a death so surprising that it became a key motivator to starting the Columbus Experiment.

Among the famous and famously connected people who have suffered or died because of typhoid are Abigail Adams, wife of President John Adams, who died of typhoid fever on October 28, 1818; and Prince Albert of Saxe-Coburg-Gotha, Queen Victoria's husband, who died on December 14, 1861.

Lincoln's first romantic interest was Ann Rutledge, whom he met when he first moved to New Salem. By 1835, they were in a relationship, though not formally engaged. She died on August 25, most likely from typhoid fever. William (Willie) Wallace Lincoln, Lincoln's third son, died February 20, 1862 of typhoid fever.

Stephen Douglas, politician and the presidential runner-up to Abraham Lincoln in 1860, died of the disease, as did Katherine McKinley, the two year-old-daughter of President William McKinley.

Wilbur Wright, one of the famous Wright Brothers, died from the disease on May 30, 1912, in Dayton, Ohio.

One individual who stands out in particular for having survived typhoid fever is Mary Mallon (1869–1938), also known as "Typhoid Mary." As a child living in Ireland, Mary successfully recuperated from the illness, but

Ohioan Wilbur Wright (1867–1912), the co-inventor of powered flight, died after being stricken with typhoid fever. *Library of Congress.*

she became an asymptomatic carrier as an adult while living in the United States. She is believed to have infected approximately fifty-three people (which resulted in three deaths) during her career as a private cook from 1900 to 1907 in the New York City area. Starting in 1900, Mary began working as a private cook, and within two weeks of her employment, the residents developed typhoid fever. She relocated to Manhattan in 1901, and members of another family for whom she worked also came down with a severe fever and diarrhea. A member of the house staff also died of typhoid fever. Quietly seeking other employment, Mallon then worked for an attorney until seven out of eight in the household came down with typhoid.

She later worked as a cook for the family of a banker named Charles Henry Warren. In the summer of 1906, the Warrens rented a house in Oyster Bay and took Mallon along as house staff. From August 27 to September 3, six of the eleven people in the home developed typhoid fever. Such an outbreak of typhoid fever in Oyster Bay was very suspicious, according to several local physicians.

Eventually, in 1907, after an intense investigation, civil health authorities were able to locate and arrest Mary Mallon. Mallon was held in isolation for three years at a clinic located on North Brother Island. After a failed attempt to return her to society, she was returned to quarantine on the island in 1915. Mallon was confined there for the remainder of her life.

CHAPTER FIVE

The Great Generation of the Nineteenth Century

As aforementioned, the Columbus Experiment was made possible by the combined contributions of many individuals to the development of America's water and wastewater infrastructure. Aside from a few award titles that carry the names of some of these individuals, these persons have mostly been forgotten and are not considered A-list celebrities in the annals of American history. It is often debated as to whether America is a country of fads and not culture. And if we take a less sophisticated view of this debate, we can see that one fad (or trend, rather) helped bring about a wide range of progress to Ohio: the post–Civil War luck or proclivity of American voting men to elect five Ohioans as president of the United States. All five had been officers in the Union army during the war and had seen the ravages of disease resulting from inadequate sanitary conditions firsthand. They served for more than half of the postwar years leading up to the twentieth century and would have held the office longer if not for the assassinations of Garfield and McKinley. The five men were: Ulysses S. Grant, the eighteenth president (1869–1877); Rutherford B. Hayes, the nineteenth president (1877–1881); James Abram Garfield, the twentieth president (1881); Benjamin Harrison, the twenty-third president (1889–1893); and William McKinley, the twenty-fifth president (1897–1901).

Unlike the big-name nineteenth-century presidents, many of the great problem solvers of that time were not embraced by historians. The forgotten men and women connected with the Columbus Experiment have not been front page news for over a century. Therefore, it seems fitting to introduce these individuals by way of a brief biography in order to more fully appreciate their work and contribution to the Columbus Experiment.

BIRDSILL HOLLY (1820–1894)

Birdsill Holly was a great American inventor, second only (in the author's opinion) to Ohio inventor Thomas Edison. Born in Auburn, New York, Holly spent most of his early years in Seneca Falls, New York. Seneca in the 1830s and '40s was a major hub for the water-powered mill industry. His first invention to receive a patent was a unique rotary water pump. But Holly's key interest was to develop a way to fight fires more efficiently.

Holly found the solution in a self-regulating water pump that would automatically provide water under pressure as needed. This pumping system made it possible to respond to sudden high or low demand for water and would quickly provide a steady stream of water to a frost-proof fire hydrant that Holly also invented. Holly convinced the city fathers of Lockport, New York, to install a test facility for his fire prevention system. He used Erie Canal water to power his pump, which pushed water through a series of iron pipes planted beneath the city streets. The fire prevention system was ready for a test in 1864. Holly had claimed that he could supply a steady stream of water through 100 feet of hose to a structure 100 feet tall. His system passed with flying colors and actually sent water flying to a height of 175 feet. To further demonstrate the seemingly limitless potential of the system, he proceeded to connect another thirteen hoses that each shot a water column simultaneously over 100 feet high.

Holly had come up with a comprehensive system for fighting fires. It was this fire protection system that brought Birdsill Holly to the attention

Birdsill Holly (1820–1894) was a great American inventor who patented a unique rotary water pump and fire hydrants. The Holly Company, depicted here, built the steam engines that powered the Columbus Water Works. *Library of Congress.*

of one very powerful investor. Thomas Flagler, the future partner of John D. Rockefeller, had originally convinced Holly to move to Lockport, New York. Following the successful demonstration, Flagler and another investor financed the new Holly Manufacturing Company. Holly Manufacturing was going to fabricate the patented Holly system for firefighting. The firm initially hired some fifty employees and started fabricating tools, jigs, patterns and the machinery needed for production. At the start of operations, they were equipped with some of the finest machinery to be found anywhere in the United States. In its prime, the company employed a staff exceeding five hundred people. The fire system was comprised of three separate Holly inventions that included a steam engine, an elliptical rotary water pump and Holly's patented fire hydrant.

Lockport, New York, was the first city to employ this system. The Holly Manufacturing Company began to install similar fire systems in cities all around the country. By 1875, the Holly Fire Protection System had been installed in over sixty cities, including Columbus, Ohio. But there were some cities that refused to purchase the Holly Fire Protection System. One of those cities was Chicago. Not long after they rejected the offer to buy this system, the Great Chicago Fire of 1871 occurred. In hindsight, this fire would have been relatively minor had they employed the Holly Fire Protection System. The City of Chicago purchased Holly's system almost immediately following the tragic fire.

Initially, Holly Manufacturing Company was powered by canal water from an aboveground raceway. As additional power was required for increased production, construction began on a new 10.5 foot underground raceway that drew water from the canal above the locks. The water then traveled through a tunnel and exited back into the canal below the locks. As the water exited the tunnel, it flowed through another one of Holly's inventions, the water-wheel turbine, producing 2,994 units of horsepower. The turbine was connected through a series of belts and pulleys to the machinery inside the factory.

Around 1870, Thomas Edison visited Holly in Lockport and asked Holly to come work with him and his associates at the Menlo Park laboratory, but Holly politely turned down Edison's offer. Also during this time, Holly sold off the rights to his fire protection system. Even though the system was a big moneymaker, it was not Holly's main focus.

One of Holly's biggest dreams was the construction of a seven-hundred-foot skyscraper. He foresaw the Niagara Falls area becoming a major tourist attraction and planned to construct his nineteen-story skyscraper on Goat

Island. He finalized his plans for his skyscraper in 1876, but he, unfortunately, had trouble finding investors for what most thought was an outlandish idea. In his lifetime, Birdsill would see skyscrapers spring up all over New York, but they were not of his design. This was perhaps his greatest defeat.

After suffering this great defeat, Birdsill Holly began work on his greatest triumph—district steam heat. After drawing up plans for his steam-heating system, he once again had trouble finding investors. Holly, however, felt so strongly about this idea that he used his own resources to finance the project. Holly chose to use his own residence at 31 Chestnut Street to demonstrate his latest invention. He first constructed a small boiler in the basement of his house. This produced the heat and is similar to modern steam and forced water furnaces. To prove he could transmit heat over long distances, he looped seven hundred feet of pipe around his backyard. On the day Holly demonstrated steam heat, a crowd of people gathered around his house in the hopes of seeing it explode. When the valve was opened, steam flowed outward. His invention worked flawlessly, and Holly's house was heated in just a matter of minutes. Investors soon lined up after word of Holly's success spread.

In 1877, the Holly Steam Combination Company was formed. For the first season of operation, mains were laid on Locust, Genesee and Walnut Streets. All were major thoroughfares in the city. When the valves were turned, thirty pounds of pressure per square inch of steam surged through the pipes, and every house and building connected to the system was heated. Once again, Holly's system performed flawlessly, and he proved his critics wrong. Other municipalities such as New York City, Long Island and Auburn also invested in steam heating that year. In 1880, the system really took off; steam heat was now being installed in cities across America. Holly also came up with a few inventions to make district steam heat more profitable. Holly suspected his customers were wasting steam because the cost was the same no matter how much they used. So, in 1881, he received a patent for an ingenious steam meter. Now customers paid for steam by volume instead of having unlimited usage. After the meters were installed, steam use was cut in half. To keep up with the growing demand for steam-heating systems, the Holly Steam Combination Company was reorganized in January 1881. It would now be known as the American District Steam Heat Company. By 1882, Holly had been issued fifty patents related to steam heat. These would be some of his last inventions.

Birdsill Holly passed away April 27, 1894 at 7:00 p.m. He had suffered from a long illness, and the cause of death was listed as heart failure.

Ironically, on the night of Holly's death, the nearby town of Gasport, New York, burned to the ground. Like Chicago, the town had not incorporated his fire hydrant system.

Thirteen years later, the Holly Manufacturing Company would be a major supplier of steam engines and pumping equipment for the Columbus Experiment.

ELLEN SWALLOW RICHARDS (1842–1911): THE FORGOTTEN TEACHER OF THE COLUMBUS EXPERIMENT ENGINEERS

Ellen Swallow Richards was the leading industrial and environmental chemist in America in the late nineteenth century. For those who think ecology is a modern crusade, it may come as a surprise that Richards concerned herself with pure water, air and food and good soil over a century ago. She was also concerned with product labeling for consumers, nutrition, industrial safety, sanitation, school lunch programs, public health and the fight for women's rights, including the right to be as well educated

Ellen Swallow Richards (1842–1911) actually instructed and mentored many of the top ranked engineers in the field of sanitary engineering in the early twentieth century. She was also responsible for developing ecology as a new science. *MIT.*

as men. She christened environmental science as Oekology, which is German for ecology.

In 1873, Richards became the Massachusetts Institute of Technology's (MIT) first female graduate. She had been a student of chemistry concentrating in applying science to the improvement of human life. She assisted in setting up a laboratory in a new discipline called "sanitary chemistry" and, in 1884, was appointed to the MIT faculty as instructor in this field. In this position, she taught the analysis of food, water, sewage and air to America's pioneer sanitary engineers who eventually set up laboratories based on her model. John H. Gregory, design engineer of the original Scioto River Water Treatment facility, and George Warren Fuller both studied sanitary chemistry under the instruction of Richards at MIT.

Richards should be especially remembered for her work in surveying the water resources for the Massachusetts State Board of Health. While at MIT, she analyzed more than 100,000 samples of the state's water and the sewerage of 83 percent of the state's population twice each month for over a two-year period. This was done while adhering to very strict clinical control standards. Her system of sample collection and delivery to the laboratory would rival today's overnight parcel services. Richards required that each sample be analyzed within a two-hour period. The project's success was due in large part to her efforts in supervising the analysis of water samples, developing new laboratory techniques, testing apparatuses and keeping records. Her sanitary survey produced the world's first purity tables and resulted in the establishment of the first state water quality standards in the United States, as well as the first sanitary chemistry laboratory. (It's worth noting this laboratory served as the model not only for other universities but also numerous state facilities and institutions in other nations.) She perfected the laboratory and constantly modified the procedures and equipment as the survey progressed.

These accomplishments resulted in the world's initial modern sewage treatment testing laboratory, the Lawrence Experiment Station located in Lowell, Massachusetts. It was staffed with several of her former students whom she personally trained, such as Allen Hazen. A few years later, a similar yet more advanced testing laboratory was built in Columbus on the lower Scioto River in 1904. It was part of the initial work of the Columbus Experiment designed by John Gregory. Clarence Hoover was hired by the city on Gregory's recommendation to be in charge of the testing lab located on the Scioto River, just south of Greenlawn Avenue.

In 1880, MIT established the first program in sanitary engineering. Richards headed the program and continued to teach successive generations

The sewage laboratory bench at the testing station. *MIT.*

of students about the analysis of water, sewage and air. She had been teaching at MIT for twenty-seven years at the time of her death in 1911, at the age of sixty-nine. Many of her students became leaders in the various disciplines of public health, sanitation and conservation.

Here in Columbus, it should be noted that engineers who were students of Richards at MIT designed the city's three supply dams. The Griggs and O'Shaughnessy Dams were both designed by John Gregory, and the Hoover dam was designed by the engineering firm of Burgess and Niple. The firm's founder, Phillip Burgess, studied sanitary engineering under Richards at MIT in the late 1890s.

GEORGE WARREN FULLER (1868–1934)

George Warren Fuller was born in Franklin, Massachusetts. After graduating MIT in 1890, he went to Germany to work in the office of C. Piefke, the chief engineer of the Berlin waterworks at the time. Upon returning to

George Warren Fuller (1868–1934) was first introduced to the science of sanitary engineering by his mentor, Ellen Swallow Richards. *PC.*

America, he began working for the Massachusetts Health Board and was soon in charge of operations at the Lawrence Experiment Station. This research station was the leading center for advancing technology in water and wastewater treatment. While there, on the recommendation of Ellen Swallow Richards, he extended an opportunity to Allen Hazen to come work with him at the Lawrence station and help develop methods for treating the increasing amounts of domestic sewage and industrial wastewater.

Fuller established an engineering consulting firm in New York in 1899 and partnered with Rudolph Hering and John Gregory. During the 1908 Columbus Experiment, Allen Hazen was particularly involved in the design of the new wastewater plant on Jackson Pike.

Allen Hazen (1869–1930)

Allen Hazen attended MIT for only two semesters in 1888 but was fortunate to study sanitary engineering under Ellen Richards. Hazen left MIT to start a new career as a sanitary chemist with the Massachusetts Health Board in Lawrence, Massachusetts. His notable record as a student of chemistry eventually qualified him to become a chemist at the Lawrence Experiment

Allen Hazen (1869–1930) was recommended to work at the Lawrence Experimental Station by his former MIT mentor, Ellen Swallow Richards. He also later consulted with John Gregory on the Columbus Experiment. *PC.*

Station. The goal of this innovative, pioneering test facility was to develop methods for treating the ever-expanding volume of sewage and industrial wastewater created by the factories and households in Massachusetts.

Hazen was directly involved in a great many civil infrastructure projects in the course of his four-decade career, including designing water treatment facilities throughout the United States, such as the wastewater plant on Jackson Pike in Columbus. His practice specialized in the full range of sewage treatment, hydraulics and potable water supply. The civil engineering practice became the predecessor to the firm Malcolm Pirnie, which continues to make modifications to the original Columbus Experiment today. In 1895, Hazen experimented with and proved the effectiveness of filtration as an effective method for purifying raw water. The initial treatment process utilized slow sand filters to provide a more aesthetic product. Within several years, filtration was recognized for removal of undesirable particles and deadly bacteria, as those communities that utilized it had fewer outbreaks of typhoid. In addition to significantly advancing the efficiency of water filtration, Hazen's contributions also included improvements in the application of rapid sand filters and slow sand filters. Both of these processes were adopted as part of the Columbus Experiment.

JERRY O'SHAUGHNESSY SR.

Jerry O'Shaughnessy Sr. was superintendent of Columbus' waterworks department for nearly twenty years and an employee of that department for nearly half a century. O'Shaughnessy was born in Delaware, Ohio, in April 1853, but lived in Columbus nearly all his life. Because of the humble circumstances of his family, he secured a very meager education. He entered the waterworks department in May 1870 as a laborer, working on the foundation of the first pumping station on Dublin Avenue. After the completion of the West Side Pumping Station, O'Shaughnessy was made wiper of machinery when the station opened in 1871 and, in six months, was promoted to fireman. He then studied engineering and, within six months, was appointed engineer, a position he filled for seventeen years until he resigned in order to take a job as an engineer at the new Wyandotte building.

He was appointed superintendent of the waterworks in 1896 by Cotton Allen and then mayor of Columbus, serving until 1899. He was removed for political reasons and succeeded by Samuel J. Schwartz. At the close of Schwartz's term, O'Shaughnessy was reappointed by Mayor John H. Hinkle and remained through the administrations of Robert H. Jeffrey and DeWitt C. Badger. Following the 1901 election, O'Shaughnessy was reappointed superintendent of the City of Columbus Water and Sewer Department. His annual report to the City's administration contained numerous comments relative to the "state of chaos," disorganization and inadequacy of the utility due to the City's inability to provide an adequate supply of water to the general public.

O'Shaughnessy's greatest contribution as a utility administrator was his ability to obtain cooperation and assemble talented individuals, such as the Hoover Brothers, for the purpose of improving and expanding the water supply and distribution infrastructure for a growing Central Ohio.

A young Jerry O'Shaughnessy started working for the waterworks in 1871 after helping dig the building's foundations. He later became a successful funeral director in Columbus as well as superintendent of the waterworks. *CML.*

CHAPTER SIX
Firefighting Versus Disease

A WATER SUPPLY FOR FIREFIGHTING

It is ironic that water is used to fight fires that can easily devastate an entire community and, at the same time, be a source that introduces disease and promotes devastating epidemics. But fire has been known to extinguish the ravages of plague epidemics.

The Great Plague (1664–66) was the last major epidemic of the bubonic plague to occur in England. This epidemic killed an estimated 100,000 people, approximately one-fifth of London's population at that time. Plague cases continued at a modest pace until September 1666, when the Great Fire of London destroyed much of the central city of London. At about the same time, the plague outbreak tapered off. The fire appears to have disinfected and rid the community of black rats that carried the Oriental rat fleas and were regular passengers on merchant ships from the east. Some believe that this was a case where disease was eradicated by fire.

Following the Great Fire of 1666, fire brigades were formed by insurance companies. The government was not involved until 1865, when these brigades became London's Metropolitan Fire Brigade. The first modern standards for the operation of a fire department were not established until 1830 and were first established in Edinburgh, Scotland. These standards outlined, for the first time, what was expected of a good fire department. After a major fire in Boston in 1631, the first fire regulation in America was established. Fire wardens were appointed in New Amsterdam (now New

York) in 1648, and this laid the groundwork for implementing the first public fire department in North America.

All too often, good sources of water for firefighting were unavailable or in short supply. A fire hydrant (sometimes called a fire plug or a Johnny pump in New York City because late nineteenth century firefighters were called Johnnies) is a fire protection device that provides a source of water in most urban, suburban and rural areas with a municipal water utility. This enables firefighters to tap into the municipal water supply to assist in extinguishing a fire. It is thought that a fire in a building near a hydrant should be more rapidly extinguished.

The concept of a fire plug dates (as far back as historical record can tell) to the seventeenth century. This was a time when firefighters responding to a call would dig down to the wooden water mains and hastily bore a hole to secure water to fight fires. The water would fill the hole and create a temporary well. It was then transported from the well to the fire by bucket brigades or by a hand-pumped fire engine. The holes were then plugged with stoppers, normally made of redwood, and over time, these came to be known as fire plugs. The location of the plug would often be recorded or marked so that it could be reused in future fires. After the Great Fire of London, the city installed water mains with holes drilled at intervals and equipped with risers, allowing an access point to the wooden fire plugs from street level.

The invention of a post- or pillar-type fire hydrant is generally credited to Frederick Graff Sr., chief engineer of Philadelphia's waterworks department, and was developed around the year 1801. It had a combination hose-faucet outlet and was of "wet barrel" design with the valve in the top. Graff was the superintendent and engineer in charge of Fairmount's waterworks department until his death in 1847. During his forty-two year tenure, Graff's many inventions and system improvements set a standard of excellence for water authorities around the world. It is said that Graff held the first patent for a fire hydrant, but this cannot be verified because the patent office in Washington, D.C., ironically caught on fire in 1836, destroying many patent records from that period in the process.

As mentioned earlier, Birdsill Holly invented the modern version of the fire hydrant. While Holly was only one of many involved in the development of the fire hydrant, innovations he introduced are largely responsible for the fire hydrant being taken for granted today. In 1869, Holly was issued U.S. patent #94749, for an "improved fire hydrant."

Generally, a hose is attached to a fire hydrant, and the valve is opened to provide a powerful flow of water, measuring between fifty and seventy-five pounds per square inch on average. This pressure varies according to region and depends on various factors, including the size and location of the attached water main. This hose can be further attached to a fire engine, which can then use a powerful pump to boost the water pressure and possibly split it into multiple streams. The hose may be connected with a threaded connection or a "quick" connector. Care should be taken not to open or close a fire hydrant too quickly, as this can create a water hammer that can damage nearby pipes and equipment. The water inside a charged hose line causes it to be very heavy, and high water pressure causes it to be stiff and prevents water from making a tight turn while pressurized. When a fire hydrant is unobstructed, this is not a problem, as there is enough room to adequately position the hose.

Municipal services, such as street sweepers and tank trucks, may also be allowed to use hydrants to fill their water tanks. Sewer maintenance truckers often need water to flush out sewage lines and fill their tanks on site from a hydrant. If necessary, the municipal workers will record the amount of water they used or use a meter.

Fire hydrants are the most accessible parts of a water distribution system, and in areas subject to freezing temperatures, only a portion of the hydrant is above ground. The valve is located below the frost line and connected by a riser to the above-ground portion. A valve rod extends from the valve itself up through a seal at the top of the hydrant, where it can be operated with the proper wrench. This design is known as a "dry-barrel" hydrant, so called because the barrel or vertical body of the hydrant is normally dry. A drain valve underground opens when the water valve is completely closed; this allows all water to drain from the hydrant body to prevent the hydrant from freezing.

Both wet- and dry-barrel hydrants typically have multiple outlets. Wet barrel hydrant outlets are typically individually controlled, while a single stem operates all the outlets of a dry-barrel hydrant simultaneously. Thus, wet barrel hydrants allow single outlets to be opened, requiring somewhat more effort but simultaneously allowing more flexibility.

A typical U.S. dry-barrel hydrant has two smaller outlets and one larger outlet. The larger outlet is known as a "steamer" connection because they were once used to supply steam-powered water pumps, and a hydrant with such an outlet may be referred to as a "steamer hydrant," although this usage is becoming archaic. Likewise, an older hydrant without a steamer connection may be referred to as a "village hydrant."

FIRE DEPARTMENTS IN THE UNITED STATES

In many ways, the early purpose of a waterworks was to provide ample water for fighting fires that could potentially destroy an entire community and local economy such as Chicago. For this reason the quality of the water was not the highest priority. In the modern sense, fire departments constitute a comparatively recent development. Their personnel are either volunteer (nonsalaried) or career (salaried). Typically, volunteer firefighters are found mainly in smaller communities while career firefighters are mainly found in cities. Having a department with salaried personnel and standardized equipment became an integral part of municipal administration only late in the nineteenth century.

Fire-alarm systems came into existence with the invention of the telegraph. Starting in the 1890s, many communities were served either with the telegraph-alarm system or with telephone call boxes. Today, most fires, however, are reported from private telephones. All alarms are then transmitted to the fire stations. Typically, on a first alarm, more personnel are sent to industrial sections, schools, institutions and theaters than to neighborhoods of one-family dwellings. Additional personnel, volunteer or off-duty, are called as needed. Fires that cannot be brought under control by the apparatus responding to the first alarm are called multiple-alarm fires, with each additional alarm bringing more firefighters and apparatus to the scene.

The early waterworks pump stations also received an alarm along with the fire station. This was to alert the pump station staff that there would be a need for an increase in water pressure. This additional pressure was called "fire pressure" and was to ensure that there was an adequate supply of water to fight the fire while maintaining sufficient pressure to keep the general community pressure from dropping.

Water is the most common fire-extinguishing agent used due to its abundance, low cost and effectiveness. Knowing what constitutes an adequate supply of water for firefighting is also central to planning fire service operations. The provision of water for firefighting operations is a significant infrastructure cost borne by the community as the firefighting requirements dominate the sizing of the water distribution network elements.

The provision of sufficient firefighting water is to ensure the fire service can curtail and suppress a fire. This requires identification of the likely size of the fire so that the fire service is able to supply enough water. The amount of firefighting water needs to be specified by pressure, flow rate and total available quantity. Although water is inexpensive and readily available, its processing and distribution carries a significant cost in terms of infrastructure. The main component of this cost is in the capital works required to treat and filter raw water to produce a potable water supply.

Fire services across America in the late nineteenth century had a major problem ensuring that there was an adequate water supply for firefighting. Too few departments seemed to address this or naively assumed that others were looking after it. This was not unique to career or volunteer departments, nor was it a rural versus urban problem. The challenges were different, but the underlying truth was the same in that too few departments were managing water supplies for firefighting. And too often, the actual buildings were firetraps waiting to happen while being ignored by the public in general. Many times, that included the local fire department.

The City of Columbus had no doubt that it was on the right track in improving its water utility after the great San Francisco earthquake of April 18, 1906, and the conflagration that followed, leaving a major portion of the city in ashes. Few people remember that most of the damage resulted from the ensuing fires and not the quake itself. This was probably the worst fire in the history of the United States. More than three hundred water main breaks and over twenty-three thousand broken water services turned the water distribution system into a sieve and reduced water pressure to the downtown area. Four days later, by the time the fire was finally extinguished on April 21, all of the city's downtown area was destroyed. Twenty-five thousand homes and commercial buildings were destroyed by fire, nearly 80 percent of the entire city's property value. It was the sixth time since 1849 that the city had burned to the ground.

The 1906 earthquake crippled the city's water supplies and left firefighters literally drafting from sewers in an effort to halt the conflagration. The people of San Francisco blamed the destruction of the city on the failed water system. Insurance rates soared, and in some areas, coverage was unobtainable.

In 1908, Marsden Manson, the San Francisco City Engineer, conducted a study of 250 cities throughout the world to develop plans for a guaranteed water-supply system for the sole purpose of fire protection. Exhaustive tests of pipe materials, valves and hydrants were conducted, and many eminent engineers of the period were consulted, many of whom also worked on the Columbus Experiment, such as Allen Hazen. All arguments were for a separate fire combat water system and against a private system outside the jurisdiction of the fire department.

The Columbus Experiment was made possible because the political bickering and arguments stopped, and common sense kicked in by virtue of the public's insistence. Once the public realized that they had the power to demand not to live with the fear of disease and fire, things began to happen. But there were still many lessons to be learned in communities that had not matured in knowledge regarding their ability to affect the general public's welfare.

Communities with fire hydrants to provide water for firefighting frequently fell victim to a tragic fire because of a false confidence that went with having a public water utility. In other words, just because a town had hydrants available didn't mean that the town had the skill, equipment and other resources required to efficiently fight a fire of any size. And all too often, fire safety was not taken seriously by the designers or managers of schools, foundries and multistory commercial buildings. What follows are several results of such malfeasance toward the public's welfare.

One reason for the Columbus Experiment's objective of expanding the city's water supply was the hard and unforgiving lessons learned from the deadly fires in other major cities. Due to the lack of building codes or the unenforcement of those codes, fires often occurred as a result of gross negligence on behalf of architects, contractors, building inspectors, building managers and owners.

The Iroquois Theatre fire that occurred on December 30, 1903, in Chicago, Illinois, is a perfect case. The Iroquois was a brand new state-of-the-art building, but the fire that broke out was the deadliest theater fire and the deadliest single-building fire in United States history. At least 605 people died as a result of the fire, and not all the deaths were reported; some of the bodies were removed from the scene prior to being recorded.

The Iroquois Theatre was located on West Randolph Street between State Street and Dearborn Street. The syndicate that financed the construction chose the location specifically to attract out-of-town ladies who were on day trips in the Loop shopping district. It was reasoned that out-of-towners would feel safer and be more comfortable attending a theater located in an area with high-profile police patrols. The theater opened in November 1903 after labor disputes and project architect Benjamin Marshall's inability to complete the required drawings delayed the project. The building was hailed by some as the most elegant theater in Chicago when it opened, and few theaters in America rivaled the Iroquois' architectural perfection.

The theater had three audience levels. The main floor was on the same level as the Grand Stair Hall. The second level and the third level were accessed through broad stairways that led off the foyer. The backstage areas were unusually large, with dressing rooms on five levels, an uncommonly large gallery where scenery was hung and even an elevator available to transport actors down to the stage level.

Despite being billed as "absolutely fireproof" in advertisements and playbills, numerous deficiencies in fire readiness were apparent, and these deficiencies were noted well before the fire. An editor of *Fireproof Magazine* had toured the building during construction and noted "the absence of an intake or stage draft shaft" and the inadequate provision of exits in his write-up, among other things. A captain with the Chicago Fire Department who performed an unofficial inspection of the theater days before the official opening noted that the theater did not have any extinguishers, sprinklers, alarms, telephones or water connections. In fact, the only firefighting equipment on site consisted of six canisters of a dry chemical, traditionally used to douse residential chimney fires. The fire department captain brought the deficiencies to the attention of the theater's fire warden and was told that nothing could be done; the fire warden would simply be dismissed if he brought the matter up with the syndicate of owners. When the captain reported the matter to his commanding officer, he was once again told nothing could or would be done because the theater already had a fire warden and the issue was his responsibility.

In addition, there were some critical design and operation deficiencies. Large iron gates blocked off the stairways during performances to prevent patrons from moving down from the gallery to better seats in the dress circle or orchestra. Many of the exit routes were confusing. Skylights on the roof of the stage, which were intended to open automatically during a fire to vent the heat and smoke, were fastened closed.

On December 30, 1903, the Iroquois Theatre presented a matinee performance of the popular musical *Mr. Bluebeard*, which had been playing at the Iroquois since opening night. The play featured American actor, comedian, dancer and vaudevillian Eddie Foy Sr. (1856–1928). Attendance since opening night had been disappointing because poor weather, labor unrest and other factors had kept playgoers away. But the December 30 performance drew a full house: every seat was filled, and hundreds of patrons filled the "standing room" areas at the back of the theatre. Many of the estimated two thousand patrons attending the matinee were children. The standing room areas were so crowded that some patrons opted to sit in the aisles, blocking the exits.

At about 3:15 p.m., the second act had just begun, opening with a dance. Suddenly, an arc light shorted and ignited a muslin curtain. A stagehand attempted to douse the fire with the dry chemical canisters provided, but the fire quickly spread to the gallery high above the stage where thousands of square feet of highly flammable painted canvas scenery flats were hung. The stage manager attempted to lower the fire curtain, but it snagged. The fire curtain was mainly made of wood pulp mixed with asbestos and would have served no real value in controlling the fire.

Foy, who was preparing to go on stage at the time, ran out and attempted to calm the crowd, first making sure his young son was in the care of a stagehand. He later wrote, "It struck me as I looked out over the crowd during the first act that I had never before seen so many women and children in the audience. Even the gallery was full of mothers and children." Foy's role in this disaster was recreated by Bob Hope in the film *The Seven Little Foys*. Foy was widely seen as a hero after the fire for his courage in remaining on stage and pleading with patrons not to panic even as large chunks of burning scenery landed around him. Architect Frank Lloyd Wright's mother-in-law and his two sons escaped unharmed.

By this time, many of the patrons on all levels were quickly attempting to exit the theater. Some had located the fire exits hidden behind draperies on the north side of the building but found that they could not open the unfamiliar bascule lock. One door was opened by a man who had a bascule lock in his home, and two others were opened either by brute force or by a blast of air, but most of the other doors could not be opened. A number of patrons panicked and began crushing or trampling others in a desperate attempt to escape the blaze. Some perished while trapped in dead-end corridors or while attempting to open windows that were designed to look like doors.

The stage performers were also forced to flee along with the performers backstage and in the numerous dressing rooms. Many escaped the theater through the coal hatch and through windows in the dressing rooms, while others attempted to escape via the west stage door, which opened inward and became jammed as actors pressed toward the door frantically trying to get out. By chance, a passing railroad agent happened to see the crowd pressing against the door and undid the hinges from the outside using tools he normally carried with him, allowing the actors and stagehands to escape. Someone opened the huge freight doors in the north wall, normally used for scenery, allowing "a cyclonic blast" of cold air to rush into the building and create an enormous fireball. As the vents above the stage were nailed or wired shut, the fireball instead traveled outward, ducking under the stuck asbestos curtain and streaking toward the vents behind the dress circle and gallery fifty feet away. The hot gases and flames passed over the heads of those in the orchestra seats and incinerated everything flammable in the gallery and dress circle levels, including patrons still in those areas. Those in the orchestra section were able to exit into the foyer and out the front door, but those in the dress circle and gallery who escaped the fireball were unable to reach the foyer because the iron grates that barred the stairways were still in place. The largest death toll was at the base of these stairways, where hundreds of people were trampled, crushed or asphyxiated.

Patrons who were able to escape via the emergency exits on the north side found themselves on the unfinished fire escapes. Many jumped or fell from the icy, narrow fire escapes, and the bodies of the first jumpers broke the falls of those who followed them. Bodies piled up around the doors and windows. Many patrons had clambered over piles of bodies only to succumb themselves to the flames, smoke and gases. An estimated 575 people died on the day of the fire; more than 30 others died the following weeks from injuries sustained in their attempts at escape.

As a result of this devastating fire, many theaters eliminated standing room. Building and fire codes were subsequently reformed, and theaters were closed for retrofitting all around the country and in some cities in Europe. All theater exits had to be clearly marked and the doors rigged so that, even if they could not be pulled open from the outside, they could be pushed open from the inside.

After the fire, it was alleged that fire inspectors had been bribed with free tickets to overlook code violations. The mayor ordered all theaters in Chicago closed for six weeks after the fire. Public outrage led to many being charged with crimes, but most of the charges were dismissed three years later. This was because of the delaying tactics of the owners' attorneys and their use of loopholes and inadequacies in the city's building and safety ordinances. The only person convicted was a tavern keeper, who was charged with robbing the dead. By 1907, thirty families of the victims had been financially compensated for their loss, receiving a settlement of $750 each, roughly $19,000 in today's currency.

In the aftermath of the catastrophic Iroquois Theatre Fire, there was a nationwide push to upgrade buildings with a safer means of egress. The Iroquois fire prompted widespread implementation of the panic bar, first invented in the United Kingdom following the Victoria Hall disaster. Panic exit devices are now required by building codes for high-occupancy spaces and were mass manufactured in the U.S. by the Von Duprin Company. Official regulations required that doors open from the inside and swing outward. This then allowed a pushing crowd to exit, but this practice did not become national until the Collinwood School Fire of 1908.

Another unfortunate example would be the Rhoads Opera House, located in Boyertown, Pennsylvania, which caught fire on January 13, 1908 during a church-sponsored stage play. The fire started when a kerosene lamp was knocked over, igniting gasoline from a stereoscopic machine. The stage and auditorium were located on the second floor, and all auxiliary exits were either unmarked or locked. One fire escape was available but could not be accessed through a locked window above a three-foot sill. A total of 171 people perished when they crowded against an exit door that opened into the hallway and prevented the door from being opened. In a number of cases, entire families were killed in this fire incident.

Closer to Columbus, the Collinwood School fire, also known as the Lake View School fire, occurred on Ash Wednesday, March 4, 1908. It was one of the deadliest disasters of its type in the United States. A total of 172 students, 2 teachers and 1 rescuer were killed in the conflagration.

Although the Lake View School was constructed as a four-story building with load-bearing exterior masonry walls, most structural floor systems used wooden joists instead of reinforced concrete. The building's main staircase extended from the front doors of the building, up to the third floor, without benefit of fire doors for exits. The stairwell acted like a chimney, helping to spread the fire and lethal smoke more quickly, and it didn't help that the oiled wooden hall and classroom floors also fueled the fire.

A common misconception about the building's design was that the doors opened inward. They did not, as has been verified in accounts of the fire written at the time. Doors to the building were equipped with common door knob latches, not modern crash bar latches. Fear and panic among students led to the crushing of many in the stairwell and the vestibules, contributing to the death toll. Students also died as a result of smoke inhalation and the fire itself. Some children died after desperately jumping from the second- and third-story windows. Members of the community could only watch as victims trapped in the building were burned far beyond recognition.

The town of Collinwood had a twenty-man fire department, but when the fire started, the horse team was about a mile away from the station, grading a road. By the time the firefighters arrived at the scene, they found a crowd of parents outside the building. The fire chief was out of town, which added to the confusion. A number of additional disappointments soon became apparent. To begin with, the gasoline-operated booster pump was too weak to place water above the first floor. One reason was that the fire hoses were old and leaky. Additionally, the firefighters' ladders were too short to reach the second floor. Axes would have been handy to take partitions entirely out, but axes were not a part of the company's standard equipment.

When the local police chief received the news by telephone, he commandeered a civilian vehicle and made his way to the fire site. There, he found that he had to guard the firefighters from the crowd. The scene had turned ugly, and bystanders were fighting firefighters, police and even each other. The police chief then enlisted some members of the crowd, whom the newspapers described as "cooler heads," to help him provide security and maintain order.

The bodies of people killed in the blaze that were not identified, as well as those students whose parents could not afford a funeral, were taken to Cleveland's Lake View Cemetery and buried in a mass grave. Additionally, several families who lost children in the fire and had the means to afford a funeral still chose to bury their children's remains adjacent to the mass grave of Collinwood victims. The Ohio General Assembly allocated $25,000 to cover the cost of burials, and the Collinwood Board of Trade supplied an additional $3,000.

The finger-pointing continued. The city council was blamed for tabling a motion to upgrade the fire department while the school board was blamed for the overcrowding in the school and for poorly planned and executed fire drills. The architects had recommended three fire escapes, but to control cost, the school board had installed only one. Additionally, the townspeople were blamed for voting down annexation and bond issues. The outcome of the inquiry, though, was that no person or agency could be held accountable under existing laws and regulations and that the cause of death was the students' own panic. Meanwhile, in Columbus, the city made a point of increasing the number of hydrants as part of the 1908 Columbus Experiment capital improvement project.

Following the fire, the remains of the Lake View School were demolished and a memorial garden planned for the site. A new school that was a fire-safe building was erected in 1911 and named the Collinwood Memorial Elementary School. This school was built adjacent to the disaster site and incorporated many features that had been lacking in the previous building. Unlike the building involved in the disaster, the new school incorporated fire safe stairwells and a central alarm system and was built with steel frames and other fire-safe materials. Although the new school was torn down in 2004, a memorial plaque remains on the site and a new development is currently being added to the area.

In the aftermath of the catastrophic Iroquois Theatre Fire, official regulations required that doors now open from the inside and swing outward, thereby facilitating public exit. The installations of what were called "panic bar" latches were mandated for doors in schools. The final casualty of the fire was the independence of the Collinwood community itself. Unable to sufficiently guarantee fire safety and firefighting resources for its residents, voters approved an annexation of Collinwood into Cleveland almost two years after the fire.

CHAPTER SEVEN

New Pump Stations, an Electric Plant and Other Equipment

A dam H. McAlpine, a chief engineer and superintendent between the years 1886 and 1895, moved the Columbus Water Works into the modern age in the latter part of the nineteenth century. McAlpine was born in Scotland on January 4, 1851. His family immigrated to the United States in 1869 when he was eighteen years old. After moving to Columbus in 1872, he took the position of a master mechanic at the Columbus Rolling Mill Company. In 1886, McAlpine accepted the position of waterworks superintendent. Due to the rapid growth of Columbus, McAlpine designed and placed into service two new pump stations during his tenure. The first facility was the Olentangy River Station in 1889, which was commonly referred to as the West Side Pumping Station. The second was the East Side Pumping Station near Alum Creek, which is just off Nelson Road across from Bexley. This station was completed and placed in service in 1891.

The new East Side Pumping Station cost $250,000 ($4,807,000 today) and had two 75-million-gallon Gaskill Triple Expansion Pumping Engines. These pumps were built by the Holly Manufacturing Company. McAlpine secured the services of two local mechanical engineers to perform the capacity and duty test on the new station. Their names were Robert B. Collier and his young assistant, Samuel P. Bush. On July 21, 1891, during the duty test run, the station received a fire alarm from a local fire engine house. The engine increased pumping pressure to compensate for fighting the fire. At the end of the fire the engine was found to have functioned smoothly and without overheating. Samuel P. Bush, twenty-eight years old at

Above: The Italianate architectural style of the East Side Water Pumping Station showed just how far the waterworks had come in just twenty years. Samuel P. Bush assisted with the initial duty test of this station when it was first placed in service in 1891. *CDW.*

Right: In 1891, Samuel Prescott Bush, at age twenty-eight, assisted the evaluating engineer who carried out the initial duty test on the new Alum Creek East Side Water Pumping Station on Nelson Road. His grandson and great-grandson would later serve as U.S. presidents. *CML.*

Picture of a horizontal Gaskill Triple Expansion Pumping Engine that was used in the Old East Side and West Side Water Pumping Stations until 1908. These engines were also built by the Holly Manufacturing Company. *CDW.*

the time, later went on to become the general manager of Buckeye Steel and a community leader in Columbus, Ohio. Years, later both his grandson and great-grandson would become president of the United States.

McAlpine later became president and manager of the Hersey Manufacturing Company in Dedham, Massachusetts, known for producing rotary water meters for national distribution. The East Side Pumping Station was taken out of service with the start-up of the new 1908 pump station on Dublin Road and was eventually demolished after World War II to make way for an expansion of the Municipal Power and Light plant.

A few years after the East Side Pumping Station was placed in service, there remained one significant problem. The quality of the water being pumped from these new facilities was fine for fighting fires but not safe for human consumption. This was due to the various small villages and towns like Westerville and Worthington that discharged raw sewage into Alum Creek and the Olentangy River. The sewerage discharged into the water

Raw water pump in the old West Side Water Pumping Station near the river confluence. *CDW.*

supply was causing contamination that resulted in a number of typhoid epidemics in the late 1800s. By 1895, the distribution system was made up of 149 miles of cast iron water pipe, 1,081 hydrants for firefighting and 1,403 water meters. By 1899, there were 177 miles of water mains, and service connections totaled 13,924. And the system was still growing.

Water bills, or water rents, as they were referred to, were paid semiannually on the first days of May and November at the main waterworks office located in the old city hall building on State Street (the present site of the Ohio Theater). Columbus residents would receive a handsome 10 percent discount if their rate bill payment was made before the twenty-fifth of the month. If water service was curtailed due to nonpayment, the customer was charged $1.00 as a turn-off fee. In order to have the service restored, an additional $3.00 had to be paid and a new service contract established as if it were a new account. In these early days, all transactions were handwritten. The charges for water service varied according to use and were per annum.

The Old Columbus City Hall on State Street housed Jerry O'Shaughnessy's office and the waterworks administration records until it was destroyed by fire in January 1921. The Ohio Theater building is now at this site. *CML.*

In 1897, banks were charged $10.00 per annum; bakeries $10.00 to $30.00; and restaurants $5.00 to $30.00. Residence with horse stables were billed per stall up to six stalls at a cost of $2.00 per stall; vehicles washed by hand were $0.75 and $1.50 if washed by hose. A church with a steam engine to operate the church organ received a special charge of $0.10 per 1,000 gallons, half the normal rate for water.

In the early years, Columbus water customers were on a first-name basis with the division's one in-house service clerk (called the customer service representative) at city hall on State Street. Water-meter readers walked a route and the inspector (there was only one) drove through neighborhoods first, using a horse and wagon (transportation was updated to a Model T Ford around 1910). In 1913, the division invested in a state-of-the-art motorized pipe thawing apparatus that was mounted on the back of a Model T Ford pickup truck and was in service for more than twenty years.

Between 1890 and 1910, the municipal works began to really develop. Columbus' first operable lighting system was demonstrated at the offices of the *Ohio State Journal* newspaper in the early 1880s. A number of private electric utility companies were established, including the Columbus Edison Electric Light and Columbus Electric Light & Power. In addition to supplying homes and businesses, these companies also provided electric street lighting, a true symbol of progress.

It cost over $70,000 a year in 1896 to provide the city with street lighting. After a feasibility study, it was determined that Columbus should operate its own street lighting system. The voters agreed by approving a bond sale to fund the construction of a new state-of-the-art, city-owned electric-generating power plant. This would give the city the coveted control of

The 1899 electric-generating power plant was a big triumph for Columbus and gave the city the ability to power most of its own street lights. *CDW.*

lighting the streets in the expanding capital city. As usual, a lack of consensus among city council members delayed the project for a few short years. But the new mayor, Samuel Black, kept his promise to the public that the electric power plant would be completed. Columbus' own electric-generating plant was placed in service in 1899 and was powered by a 264-horsepower engine. Still, a number of street lights continued operating on private service for a few years because the amount of energy consumed by the use of arc lamps limited the capacity of the new plant.

Columbus became known as the "City of Arches" after the city power works assumed control of the illuminated decorative arches on High Street in 1909. Years later, the arches would fade away as an archaic symbol of a bygone era, only to appear again when the restored area became known as the Short North district. A year later, the city electric division began supplying power to public buildings and commercial businesses in the downtown area. City hall and the new waterworks on Dublin Road were among the first establishments to receive power. Earlier customers were Grant Hospital, the new Carnegie Library on Grant Street and various drugstores, hardware stores and church buildings.

CHAPTER EIGHT

The Need for a Dam

By the end of the 1890s, having a long-term water-supply system for future decades became a necessity. The previous groundwater supply that was derived from the gravel beds of Alum Creek, on the eastern side of the city, and from similar areas of saturated gravel on both sides of the Scioto River had apparently reached the limit of exploitation.

Though McAlpine helped to revolutionize the waterworks system mid-century, city engineer Julian Griggs would be the man to move the Columbus Water Works into the early twentieth century. Julian Griggs was born September 15, 1848, in Chaplin, located in Windam County, Connecticut. He attended the Sheffield Scientific School at Yale University and came to Columbus in 1880. Mr. Griggs served as a division engineer for the Norfolk & Western Railroad prior to being appointed city engineer in 1893 by mayor George J. Karb.

The central Ohio region experienced a severe drought in the autumn of 1895 and 1897, and very little had been done to increase the general supply of water for the community. In 1898, Griggs invited a California construction hydrological engineer named James D. Schuyler to inspect a site and prepare a report regarding a proposed water-supply storage dam. Schuyler conducted a thorough and comprehensive inspection of a site some seven miles above the city proposed for the storage dam on the Scioto River. In addition, his report provided feedback on the feasibility of a preliminary design for a Scioto River dam drawn up by Griggs.

Schuyler's report stated that there was no question that there was a need for the dam in order to secure a more than adequate provision for the future.

The 1889 West Side Water Pumping Station on Old Dublin Avenue near the river confluence. *CDW.*

And even though a new forty-two-inch cast iron, perforated conduit was being put in place, it would only yield a marginal increase in groundwater volume. This delayed the immediate necessity of taking raw water directly from the surface flow of the Scioto River to eke out the supply during the dry season. Although expedient, this was a very undesirable solution that had been resorted to in the past but only added an additional 12–15 percent of the entire volume consumed by the public and local industry, such as the railroads.

Following his ground inspection, Schuyler was convinced that the areas of gravel available for yielding water were too limited to be depended upon much longer for the needs of a city the size of Columbus. The natural encroachment of the population near and upon the land area where the drainage constitutes the chief source of water supply on both sides of the Scioto River was becoming the source of contamination and a growing pollution menace. The time was rapidly approaching when the entire supply would need to be artificially purified and filtered and when stored water would be the sole resource because of the contamination of all the groundwater now drawn upon by the conduits of the West Side Pumping Station at the river confluence. The most expedient solution would be to

John Kilroy (standing on the far right), chief engineer of the West Side Pumping Station, and his staff in 1898. *PC.*

concentrate the pumping works at one location and supply the entire city from the artificial filter beds that could be most advantageously located below and near the proposed dam.

Maintaining the Alum Creek Pumping Station as a water-supply source wasn't a likely prospect. The Alum Creek water was excessively hard, charged with the carbonates and sulfates of lime and magnesia and had a marked amount of iron protoxide, which rapidly formed deposits of hydrated-iron oxide, giving water a rust color.

Schuyler made a point of saying that until a new filtration plant was constructed, the stored water would be a necessity to reinforce the groundwater supply, which was obtained through percolation of the Scioto River bed and its banks. The probability that the new filtration system would be depended upon for all water consumed had to be considered in planning the construction of the dam, especially in regards to its height. This also meant that the dam needed to be built immediately.

Schuyler also noted that the greater the average depth of the dam's reservoir, the better the quality of the water would be. Additionally, the report cited the long distance through which the water must travel from the point of entry to its exit at the dam as an excellent feature in constructing the system. This would allow a greater portion of the sediment carried by the stream at the upper end and would also render the water much clearer before it entered the filter beds. According to the report, this should be the case at every stage of the dam on the river, and even in the highest floods, the velocity would be so checked as to compel the current to drop the bulk of its load at the upper end of the reservoir.

The report suggested that a future study be made by observations and taking samples to help further answer the question regarding sedimentation, which was very important for a reservoir. If the load of sediment was not great and did not precipitate or settle rapidly and easily, it would have no serious effect upon the reservoir in the way of diminishing its capacity. On the other hand, it would be more difficult to clarify in sedimentation settling basins and filter beds. An intelligent study of these conditions was then essential in planning the new purification works. Since the City was about to take control of the river by erecting the dam, it was also highly desirable to know more of the volume of flow. This could be achieved by establishing gauging stations and river rods at convenient points and beginning a systematic recording program and taking a series of measurements.

Griggs made a point of furnishing Schuyler with a table of the estimated discharge of the Scioto River from the state dam on the Olentangy in Columbus. The table was based on previous gauging conducted over a period of fifteen months between January 1897 and March 1898. The tables indicated that the approximate total discharge of the river during the year 1897 was 33.71 billion cubic feet, and this represented a mean run-off of 23.4 percent of the precipitation. The discharge during January, February and March 1898 was 28.2 billion cubic feet, 16 percent more than the corresponding period in 1897. However, the discharge in March 1898, which covered flood discharge from a great flood, was nearly 1.0 billion cubic feet less than the total flow in March from the previous year. The Scioto above the proposed dam had a tributary watershed that totaled almost two-thirds of that draining past the state dam, and it may be assumed, in the absence of definite data, that the volume of water yielded by the upper Scioto bore a proportionate ratio to the area of its shed. Therefore, the volume of water that passed the Lakin Dam site in 1897 was approximately 22.12 billion cubic feet. This would give a mean water discharge volume of 710 cubic feet per second throughout the year if it were evenly distributed.

Schuyler used historic Central Ohio data from the Muskingum River to aide him in his report. After carefully gauging the Muskingum River in Zanesville daily for eight years, U.S. Army Captain H.M. Chittenden of the Engineer Corps determined an interesting relationship between rainfall and run-off. Chittenden deduced that the minimum supply of water in dry years affected the regimen of the reservoir and the amount of available power. The Muskingum is a stream derived from a more highly and heavily wooded watershed and is more freely supplied by living springs than the Scioto, which Chittenden classified as a "prairie stream." He estimated that the prairie class of streams in Ohio would give a run-off ranging from 4.5 to 9.0 inches in depth over its watershed per annum. On the basis of this classification, the Scioto River may be expected to discharge at the Lakin Dam site from 10.15 billion cubic feet per annum as the minimum in dry years to 20.3 billion as the maximum of average wet years. The report noted that these figures did not differ greatly from the computations made by Griggs from the gauge data collected in 1897, which indicated a total precipitation of 40.0 inches, the mean of the observed rainfall over the entire watershed.

The gentleman handling the team of horses and wagon is Mr. Billy Bundy. Bundy worked for one of the waterworks supply vendors in 1898. *CH.*

The Schuyler report also noted that the precise site for locating the proposed dam was determined by a number of soundings taken down at the bedrock in the bottom of the stream. The site had been selected following several sub-surface examinations. This is because several miles of the entire valley are filled with small particles of rock that have been worn or broken away from a mass by water or glacial ice and range from three to thirty feet in depth. This material covers the bedrock, which is not exposed in the stream channel anywhere below a point some fifteen miles from the city.

The soundings had to be taken with extreme care and thoroughness, so that the indications of rock in place were unmistakable when reached by the sounding rod. The site chosen at the Lakin Farm was 5.3 miles above the present waterworks' supply intake and, by the evidence of the soundings and measurements of width, was far superior to all the other sites. It was also a proper distance from the city to be clear of any probable spread of population for some generations to come and, at the same time, not an excessive distance for piping the water.

The design of the dam first prepared by Griggs was a thirty-foot-high structure above low water and would be built of concrete made from Portland cement. The dam was shaped to permit the entire flow of the stream to pass over its crest. Subsequently, the State Board of Health, to whom the plans were submitted upon the advice of engineer Allen Hazen, recommended that the dam be increased to a height of at least fifty feet, so that the storage would be greatly increased and the quality of water improved by the additional depth. The addition of twenty feet suggested by Hazen and the State Board of Health would have increased the reservoir capacity by three times the proposed capacity. Schuyler thought that the recommendation of added height would have been eminently wise and entirely justifiable by the corresponding advantages to be derived from maintaining a greater volume of water at higher level.

Hazen had apparently overlooked the fact that the public had not forgotten the 1889 tragedy of the dam failure at Johnstown, Pennsylvania. That fear would later compromise the actual constructed height of the dam. Looking at the foundations, Schuyler had no objections, even with the proposal that the dam be an additional 50 or 60 feet high. Schuyler regarded the limestone at the site as entirely safe and a suitable foundation for a structure of even greater height. But he did mention that it would be inadvisable to build an overfall dam made of concrete at this height since it was possible it would be subject to the shocks and strains of passing floods that might reach a maximum of 40,000 to 50,000 cubic feet per second over several hours. This condition could be avoided by the excavation of a spillway of sufficient size in the solid rock around the dam. Schuyler also felt that there was no question that good-quality concrete would resist the erosion satisfactorily if placed in the "ogee" form (designed by Griggs) and with a dam limited to the height of 30 feet as first proposed. But he continued to state in his report that he would have less confidence in the stability of a 50-foot structure because of the erosive action upon the crest and apron at maximum flooding and the impact of thousands of tons of water falling 50 feet. In this case, the additional upward pressure, caused by possible leaks underneath the dam from fissures in the bedrock or cracks in the concrete, could reduce the gravity of the mass as if it were completely immersed in water. These complex strains upon the dam could be avoided by cutting a spillway that could carry maximum flooding. The form and size of dam required would be designed to adequately resist the pressure of quiet water upon its face along with ice thrust.

Schuyler submitted his report and made these recommendations to Felix A. Jacobs, director of public improvements for the City of Columbus, and Griggs on July 26, 1898. Unfortunately, the momentum of progress associated with the report came to a halt as it moved to higher political authorities. (At this time, only men had the right to vote, and much of the voting public were saloon patrons who had no real interest in the quality of drinking water.)

In 1901, Columbus' funeral director, Jerry O'Shaughnessy, was reappointed superintendent of the water and sewer department. That same year, his annual report to the city administration contained numerous comments relative to the "state of chaos," disorganization and the inadequacy of the utility due to the inability to provide an adequate supply of water to the general public. Realizing the need to move ahead, Griggs retained civil engineer Samuel M. Gray of Providence, Rhode Island, to make a study and preparatory plans for an actual water storage dam on the Scioto River. Like Hazen, Gray had also envisioned a fifty-foot high dam structure. But the public fear of a large dam breaking and the memory of the tragic 1889 Johnstown, Pennsylvania flood put Gray's plan on hold. But it was another public tragedy that played a pivotal role in resurrecting Gray's original concept a few years later.

Johnstown, Pennsylvania, was nestled into the Appalachian Plateau River valley. The Little Conemaugh and the Stony Creek Rivers, which span the outline of the town, merged in the Conemaugh River at the western end, draining a 657-square-mile watershed. This watershed ran off into the rivers from mountains 500 feet above. At least once a year, one or both of the

Debris buildup from the Johnstown Flood of 1889. *Library of Congress.*

rivers overflowed into the community, sending the town's residents into a panic to protect their families and property.

Some flooding occurred in the spring, when heavy snows rapidly melted, and when heavy rains saturated the region. Spring flooding was a common occurrence to the residents of this nineteenth-century industrial community located in southwestern Pennsylvania. In the late afternoon of May 31, 1889, people were gathered in the upper floors of their residences, waiting for the water to subside as they had done many times in prior years.

Even as the residents of Johnstown prepared for their long wait, activity at the South Fork Dam, just fourteen miles above the city, was frantic. The South Fork Dam restrained the water of Lake Conemaugh, which was the recreational lake of the South Fork Fishing and Hunting Club, an exclusive club known for having prestigious members on its rosters, such as steel industrialist Andrew Carnegie and entrepreneur Henry Clay Frick. Fearing that the dam would fail, club officials had been working since mid-morning to avoid a dam failure because they knew full well the consequences. The lake was over two miles long and about a mile wide at its widest spot, with a depth of sixty feet at the earth dam.

First, the club attempted to add height to the dam and dig a second spillway to relieve pressure from the breast of the dam. Second, the heavy screens that had been placed on the overflows to keep the stocked fish from escaping into the streams below were opened. By mid-afternoon, most of the Johnstown residents had settled in to be stranded at home for the evening. Club officials and the workers they had recruited, along with a sizable crowd from the little town of South Fork just below the dam, watched in absolute horror as the South Fork Dam collapsed and unleashed twenty million tons of water from its reservoir. A rolling wall of water and debris that was some seventy feet high and half a mile wide swept down fourteen miles of the Little Conemaugh River valley, carrying away steel mills, houses, barns, livestock and people—both dead and alive. At 4:07 p.m., the floodwaters rushed into the industrial city of Johnstown, crushing houses and downtown businesses in a whirlpool that lasted ten minutes. Most people only heard the thunderous rumble as it swept into the city.

Some people waited out the disaster in their homes, but a number of others were picked up by the flood wave for a horrifying ride through the streets to the Pennsylvania Railroad Company's Stone Bridge, where flood debris piled forty feet high and over thirty acres of land caught on fire. Still, others were shot down the Conemaugh River to die or be rescued at Nineveh, Bolivar or other communities downstream.

Years later, one woman, Gertrude Quinn Slattery, who was six years old at the time of the flood, would write about her experience. She recalled being hurled through the torrents on what she describes as a "raft with a wet muddy mattress and bedding."

> I had great faith that I would not be abandoned. While my thoughts were thus engaged, a large roof came floating toward me with about twenty people on it. I cried and called across the water to them to help me. This, of course, they could not do. The roof was big, and they were all holding on for dear life, feeling every minute that they would be tossed to death. While I watched, I kept praying, calling and begging someone to save me. Then I saw a man come to the edge, the others holding him and talking excitedly. I could see they were trying to restrain him, but he kept pulling to get away which he finally did and plunged into the swirling waters and disappeared.
>
> Then his head appeared and I could see he was looking in my direction, and I called, cried and begged him to come to me. He kept going down and coming up, sometimes lost to my sight entirely, only to come up next time much closer to my raft. The water was now between fifteen and twenty feet deep.
>
> As I sat watching this man struggling in the water my mind was firmly fixed on the fact that he was my savior. At last he reached me, drew himself up and over the side of the mattress and lifted me up. I put both arms around his neck and held

on to him like grim death. Together, we went downstream with the ebb and flow of the reflex to the accompaniment of crunching, grinding, gurgling, splashing and crying and moaning of many. After drifting about, we saw a little white building standing at the edge of the water, apparently where the hill began. At the window were two men with poles helping to rescue people floating by. I was too far out for the poles, so the men called:

"Throw that baby over here to us."

My hero said, "Do you think you can catch her?"

They said, "We can try."

So Maxwell McAchren threw me across the water (some say twenty feet, others fifteen. I could never find out, so I leave it to your imagination. It was considered a great feat in the town, I know.)

I can never forget what I saw! It was like the Day of Judgment I have since seen pictured in books. Pandemonium had broken loose, screams, cries and people were running: their white faces like death masks; parents dragging children, whose heads bobbed up and down in water; a boat filled to capacity with eager anxious passengers; household pets of all descriptions dangling from loving arms, a wagon loaded to the breaking point lost a wheel and the despairing mortals riding therein where dumped down in a heap in the filthy water. They scrambled to their feet in less time that it takes to tell it, as the onrushing mob moved rapidly forward bent on self-protection at any cost.

Animals and humans with eyes bulging out of their heads struggled to keep their feet against the horde and the weight of the water. They were all compressed into a solid mass that fairly wedged its way up the street, all straining every nerve and muscle to reach the hill, as the grim reaper stalked in the rear, and in the distance, the mist and unmistakable rumblings telling in a new language what had happened.

Bells were ringing, the whistles in the mills were sounding a last warning and intermingled with these were the shrill sounds from steam engines as throttles were opened for the last time; and now a moving mass black with houses, trees, boulders, logs and rafters coming down like an avalanche.

The response to this 1889 disaster was immediate as over one hundred newspapers including the Columbus Dispatch and a number of magazines sent writers and illustrators to Johnstown to recount the story for the world. Although much of the reporting was not noted for its accuracy, the reports touched the hearts of the nation. The public responded by sending money, clothing and food. Medical societies, physicians and hospitals sent medicines and bandages. A few physicians temporarily left their practices and hurried to Johnstown to render their assistance. Building tradesmen came to the area, and building materials were sent for rebuilding homes and businesses.

The Need for a Dam

The bodies of the unfortunate dead were on display in several morgues throughout Johnstown and in the small communities further down the Conemaugh River. This was done in hope that some of the survivors in search of their relatives and loved ones would be able to make a positive identification. The flood-damaged Presbyterian Church located on Main Street was the site of one of the morgues and a New York Evening Post *reporter gave a detailed description of what he witnessed.*

The first floor has been washed out completely, and the second, while submerged, was badly damaged but not ruined. The walls, floors and pews were drenched and the mud has collected on the matting and carpets an inch deep. Walking is attended with much difficulty, and the undertakers and attendants, with arms bared, slide about the slippery surface at a tremendous rate. The channel is filled with coffins, strips of muslin, boards and all undertaking accessories. Lying across the top of the pews are a dozen pine boxes each containing a flood victim. Printed cards are tacked to each. Upon them, the sex and full description of the enclosed body is written with the name of the known.

The living set up tents, often where their former homes had been, and began what must have been perceived as the impossible task of cleaning up and beginning to build a new life. Clara Barton and her Washington, D.C., contingent of the Red Cross built hotels for people to live in and warehouses to store the many supplies received by the community. By July 1, stores opened on the Main Street for business. The Cambria Iron Company reopened on June 6. Five years later, an observer would have been hard pressed to imagine the destruction in the valley on May 31, 1889.

However, no city, county or state legislation was enacted to protect people from similar disasters in the future. Suits were filed against the members of the South Fork Fishing and Hunting Club, but in keeping with the times, the courts viewed the dam break as an act of God and no legal compensation was made to the survivors.

The city would continue to suffer nuisance floods as water collected in the streets and in people's basements, especially in the spring of the year. It would be another forty-seven years, after more property was destroyed and more lives lost, until some constructive efforts were made to control the waters that flowed through Johnstown. The news and stories of the Johnstown Flood continued to echo in the minds of Columbus, Ohio citizens over the next three decades whenever that subject of building a dam came up. Indeed, Johnstown's flood experience taught the people of Central Ohio a lesson in fear and mistrust of any public works project, including building a dam anywhere near the city. It most likely added to the reason city leaders in Columbus continued to talk, bicker and debate about building a badly needed water-supply dam.

CHAPTER NINE

McKinley, Hanna and Roosevelt

WILLIAM MCKINLEY (1843–1901)

William McKinley was the twenty-fifth president of the United States and served in office from March 4, 1897, until his untimely death in September 1901. He also was connected to a key catalyst of the Columbus Experiment, as he was close friends with Marcus Hanna, a U.S. senator who eventually died of typhoid. As president, McKinley raised protective tariffs to promote and secure jobs and American industry, led the nation to victory in the brief Spanish-American War and maintained the nation on the gold standard.

As a young man, McKinley served in the Union army and rose from the low rank of private to brevet major by the end of hostilities. Following the war, he returned to Ohio and settled in Canton, where he practiced law for a living. As McKinley's professional career developed, so too did his social life, and he came to court Ida Saxton, the daughter of a prominent Canton family. They were married on January 25, 1871, in Canton. Their firstborn child, Katherine, arrived on Christmas Day, 1871, and a second daughter, Ida, followed in 1873, but she unfortunately died that same year. McKinley's wife descended into a deep depression following Ida's death and, already weak, her health grew even more severe. Two years later, in 1875, Katherine died of typhoid fever. Ida McKinley never recovered from losing her daughters. Around the same time as Katherine's death, she developed epilepsy and, as a result, disliked her husband being away from her for any period of time. McKinley was deeply devoted to his wife and always took care of her medical and emotional needs for the balance of their married life. Years later, as McKinley collapsed from being hit by an assassin's bullet, he whispered to an aide, "My wife, be careful...how you tell her...Oh be careful."

William McKinley (1843–1901) was the twenty-fifth president of the United States and a former governor of Ohio. *Library of Congress.*

McKinley was elected governor of Ohio in 1891 and again 1893 and maintained a moderate affiliation between both capital and labor interests. With the aid of his close adviser, millionaire and industrialist Marcus Hanna, he secured the Republican nomination for president in 1896, amid a deep economic depression. He defeated well-known Democratic presidential candidate William Jennings Bryan after a front-porch campaign, in which he promoted the idea of "sound money" (maintaining the gold standard).

Prosperity and accelerated economic growth was the hallmark of McKinley's presidency. By promoting the 1897 Dingley Tariff, he helped protect manufacturers and labor from foreign competition, and in 1900, he secured the passage of the Gold Standard Act. Following the Spanish-American War, he secured a peace settlement with Spain that required them to cede their overseas colonies of Puerto Rico, Guam and the Philippines. The United States also undermined the independent Republic of Hawaii and annexed it in 1898 as a U.S. territory.

Marcus Alonzo Hanna (1837–1904)

Marcus Hanna was born in New Lisbon, Ohio. His parents were associated with the Society of Friends, and Hanna shared their religious beliefs, including being strongly against the institution of slavery. The Hanna family relocated to Cleveland, Ohio, in 1852. He and John D. Rockefeller were classmates in high school.

U.S. Senator Marcus Hanna's death from typhoid fever served as a catalyst that helped the Columbus Experiment move forward. *OHS.*

In the first presidential election in which Hanna voted, he cast his ballot for Abraham Lincoln. In 1864, he briefly served in the Union army as one of Ohio's Hundred Days Men. He was assigned to garrison duty in Washington, D.C., and never went into combat. Prior to leaving the military, he had earned the rank of second lieutenant. Hanna returned to Cleveland, Ohio, where he managed his father's business and also began refining oil. In 1867, his oil refinery was destroyed by fire. He then went to work for a firm involved in coal and iron mining called Rhodes & Company that was owned by his father-in-law.

Having recovered financially, Hanna invested in a shipbuilding company that built ships designed to transport freight on the Great Lakes. In 1884, Hanna skillfully established the Union National Bank and was a partner in a company that specialized in urban streetcar transportation. Once he had achieved success as a businessman, Hanna began to participate in politics and supported the Republican Party. In the years he owned the *Cleveland Herald* newspaper, Hanna made a point of publicly endorsing Republican issues. As a result, by 1887, Hanna was one of the most powerful Republicans in Ohio while having never held an elected public office.

During the late 1880s and 1890s, Hanna donated large sums of money to John Sherman and William McKinley to help them in their campaigns for public office. In 1891, Hanna's financial leverage secured McKinley's election as governor of Ohio and Sherman's reappointment to the United States Senate. But in 1894, Hanna resigned as the general manager of his numerous business concerns to focus his time on getting his friend McKinley elected to the office of president. During the 1896 election, Hanna was chairman of the Republican National Committee and spent well over $100,000 of his own funds to get McKinley nominated as the party's presidential candidate. He also established a grassroots movement to help

McKinley win the presidency. He brought pressure on businessmen across the United States and warned them that the Democratic Party's candidate, William Jennings Bryan, opposed large businesses. Hanna's efforts won McKinley the presidency. However, his actions earned him a reputation as an unscrupulous person, who favored the wealthy over the poor.

Upon becoming president, McKinley offered Hanna a position in the cabinet. Hanna refused, preferring to seek an appointment to the United States Senate. McKinley appointed Senator John Sherman as secretary of state, and this opened up a senate seat. Ohio's governor, Asa Bushnell, immediately appointed Hanna to the Senate. After a controversial vote within the Ohio legislature, Hanna was reappointed to the U.S. Senate in 1898. As a senator, Hanna was President McKinley's strongest ally in Congress.

McKinley defeated Bryan a second time in the presidential election of 1900. His campaign issues focused on imperialism, prosperity and free silver. His vice president for his second term was the forty-two-year-old Spanish-American War hero and Republican governor of New York, Theodore Roosevelt. But how did a young cowboy, as Hanna called Roosevelt, get on the ballot as vice president in the first place? As New York governor,

Last known photograph of President William McKinley, taken shortly after he arrived at the Temple of Music on Friday, September 6, 1901. He was assassinated moments later. *Library of Congress.*

Roosevelt was a serious progressive reformer. He made such a point of rooting out corruption and "old party machine politics" that the Republican Party boss, Thomas Collier Platt, forced him on President McKinley as his running mate for the 1900 election to get Roosevelt out of New York. In that era, the office of vice president was considered by many to be a dead-end career position. This move was contrary to the wishes of Senator Hanna, who was McKinley's campaign manager. Nevertheless, Roosevelt was a powerful campaign asset for the Republican ticket and helped defeat Bryan by a landslide. As fate would have it, on September 6, 1901, six months into McKinley's second term, a man name Leon Czolgosz went to the Pan-American Exposition in Buffalo, New York, where President McKinley was in attendance, carrying a .32 caliber revolver with him. With the gun wrapped in a handkerchief in his pocket, Czolgosz approached McKinley's procession. The president was standing in a receiving line in the Temple of Music, greeting the public. Czolgosz moved to the front of the line, and as the president extended his hand, Czolgosz slapped it to one side and shot McKinley twice in the abdomen at close range. Czolgosz was quickly restrained by the crowd, but before the police could intervene, he was beaten so severely that he nearly died before he was able to stand trial. Czolgosz was convicted on September 24, 1901, and was electrocuted in a prison in Auburn, New York, on October 29, 1901.

After President McKinley was assassinated in Buffalo, New York, he was succeeded by Vice President Theodore Roosevelt. This greatly upset the plans and expectations of McKinley's number one supporter, the junior senator from Ohio, Marcus Hanna. McKinley's death left Hanna devastated both personally and politically. But even after McKinley's death, Hanna remained one of the nation's most powerful Republicans. He advised the new president during the anthracite coal strike but later lost influence in the increasingly progressive administration.

Vice President Roosevelt conferring with Senator Hanna on the way to the Milburn House to see the mortally wounded President McKinley. *Library of Congress.*

Historians agree that Hanna's greatest success was getting Congress to agree on acquiring the Panama Canal. In 1903, the Ohio legislature reappointed Hanna to the Senate. Looking at the presidential election for 1904, many Republicans and industrialists strongly considered nominating Hanna for the presidency rather than Roosevelt. Several months prior to his death, Hanna withdrew from consideration and threw his support behind Roosevelt.

THEODORE "TEDDY" ROOSEVELT (1858–1919)

Theodore Roosevelt became the twenty-sixth president of the United States, serving from 1901 until 1909. He was especially noted for his exuberant personality, his wide range of interests and achievements and being the leader of the Progressive movement. As a naturalist, he was a strong promoter of the conservation movement. Together Roosevelt and Marcus Hanna were the force behind America's deciding to take over and complete the failed Panama Canal project from the French. Roosevelt won the Nobel Peace Prize for his part in negotiating an end to the Russo-Japanese War. Roosevelt improved the quality of life for the public in general by instituting laws such as the Meat Inspection Act and the Pure Food and Drug Act. The Meat Inspection Act prohibited misleading labels and banned many preservatives that contained harmful chemicals, while the Pure Food and Drug Act banned food and drugs that are impure or falsely labeled from being made, sold and shipped. It is fitting that the Columbus Experiment unfolded during Roosevelt's progressive administration.

Although the two had never been allies, as the new president, Roosevelt reached out to Hanna, hoping to gain his influence in the Senate. Hanna indicated that he was willing to come to terms with Roosevelt because the new president was willing to follow through with the McKinley agenda. Historically, Hanna would prove to be a major supporter of building a canal across Central America to allow ships to pass from the Atlantic to the Pacific Ocean without making the long tedious voyage around Cape Horn. Hanna specifically viewed the route across the Colombian province of Panama to be far superior to its Nicaraguan rival.

How he came to support this route is uncertain, but he was most likely convinced by the French canal promoter, Philippe Bunau-Varilla (1859–1940), who was also an engineer and soldier. Bunau-Varilla greatly influenced the United States' decision concerning the construction site for the famed Panama Canal after meeting with Hanna in his home at the Arlington Hotel in Washington. Bunau-Varilla also worked closely with President Roosevelt in orchestrating the very short nonviolent Panamanian Revolution, resulting in Panama's independence from Colombia. In addition, he used Hanna's influence to convince the U.S. Senate to appropriate $40 million for the New Panama Canal Company under the Spooner Act of 1902. The funds were contingent on negotiating a treaty with Colombia to provide land for the canal in its territory of Panama.

But this didn't happen without a fight. An alternate route through Nicaragua had many supporters and a bill sponsored by Iowa Congressman William Peters Hepburn, which would authorize the construction of a canal on the Nicaragua route, had passed the House of Representatives. In the U.S. Senate, Hanna made a speech against the Hepburn Bill. In making his presentation, he referred to large maps that were displayed throughout the senate chamber. He referred to the potential of active volcanoes on the Nicaragua route, and the maps showed active volcanoes marked with red dots and extinct volcanoes with black. Hanna cited the many advantages of the Panama route starting with that it was shorter than the Nicaraguan route and would require much less digging because the French had completed at least a third of the job fifteen years previously. The Panama route had existing harbors at either end. Apparently Hanna was not in the best of health while giving his speech. Alabama senator John Tyler Morgan, the senate sponsor of the Hepburn Bill, tried to ask Hanna a question, only to be met with, "I do not want to be interrupted, for I am very tired." At the end, Hanna warned that if the U.S. built the Nicaragua Canal, another power would finish the Panama route started by the French. Consequently, the bill was amended to support a Panama route, according to some accounts in part because Bunau-Varilla's lobbyist, New York attorney William Nelson Cromwell, remembered that Nicaragua depicted volcanoes on its postage stamps. He then combed the stock of Washington stamp dealers until he found enough to send to the entire Senate. The House agreed to the Senate amendment afterward, and the bill authorizing a Panama Canal passed.

In November 1903, Panama, with the support of the United States, broke away from Colombia and, with Bunau-Varilla as representative of the new Panamanian government in Washington, signed a treaty granting the U.S. a separate zone in which to build the canal. Debates over the treaty began in the Senate as Hanna lay dying. However, the United States Senate ratified the treaty on February 23, 1904, eight days following the death of fellow Senator Marcus Hanna.

McKinley, Hanna and Roosevelt

On the floor of the Ohio Republican convention in 1903, a resolution was filed and backed by several key delegates to endorse Roosevelt for reelection. This would normally have been introduced at the 1904 convention, but the plan was to use the resolution to take control of the Ohio party from Hanna. The resolution placed Hanna in a difficult position: if he backed it, he was stating that he would not run for president; if he opposed the resolution, he would risk becoming an enemy of Roosevelt. Hanna wired Roosevelt that he intended to oppose it and would explain all the details once both men were in Washington. Roosevelt responded that while he had not requested support from anyone, those friendly to his administration would naturally vote for such a statement. Hanna's bid for the presidency was undermined by his fellow Ohio Republicans and he therefore had little choice but to support the resolution.

The 1903 convention also endorsed Hanna for reelection to the Senate and nominated Hanna's friend, Myron Herrick, for governor. The Foraker faction was allowed to nominate a lieutenant governor, Warren G. Harding, who later became president. Hanna campaigned for several weeks for the Republicans in Ohio and was rewarded with an overwhelming Republican victory.

Despite strong differences between the two men, in November 1903, Theodore Roosevelt asked Marcus Hanna to run his 1904 reelection campaign. Naturally, Hanna clearly viewed this as an unsubtle attempt by Roosevelt to ensure that he would not oppose him, so Hanna took his time to respond to the president's offer. In the meantime, he allowed talk of Hanna's campaigning for president to proceed, even though he had decided not to run for the office. During this interim, the New York financial titan J. P. Morgan, who had no love for Roosevelt or his policies, made an offer to finance a presidential campaign for Hanna. Morgan extended this offer when he hosted Hanna and his wife Charlotte at Thanksgiving. But Hanna remained silent and gave no answer regarding the offer. In December, Hanna and Roosevelt had an in-depth meeting and resolved a number of their differences. Roosevelt agreed that Hanna would not have to serve another term as chairman of the Republican National Committee. This theoretically freed Hanna to run for president, but Roosevelt could clearly see that the sixty-six-year-old Hanna was a marginally healthy, tired man and would not run for the presidency.

With the New Year, Hanna returned to Columbus for Myron Herrick's inaugural ceremony as the new governor of Ohio on January 11, 1904. A "Boil the Water" alert had been in effect since January 8 because six cases of typhoid had been reported, one of which resulted in a death. While in Columbus, Hanna stayed at the Chittenden Hotel, known to serve its guests distilled water, although he usually drank mineral water.

During his visit, the *Columbus Dispatch* headlines read, "City Threatened with Epidemic of Typhoid."

Shortly after returning to Washington, D.C., Marcus Hanna became very ill. On January 30, 1904, Hanna attended the Gridiron Club dinner at the Arlington Hotel. He didn't eat or drink anything, and when someone inquired how he was feeling, he replied, "Not good." He never again left his Washington residence after being stricken with an acute case of typhoid fever. Debates over the Panama Treaty began in the Senate as Hanna lay dying. As the days passed, politicians began to wait in the Arlington Hotel lobby, close to Hanna's suite for news of his recovery. Hanna drifted in and out of consciousness for several days until on the morning of February 15, when his heart began to fail. Roosevelt visited at 3:00 p.m., unseen by the dying man. At 6:30 p.m., Senator Hanna died, and the crowd of congressional colleagues, government officials and diplomats who had gathered in the lobby of the Arlington left the hotel, many sobbing. The United States Senate ratified the Panama Treaty on February 23, 1904, eight days after Hanna's death.

One of Theodore Roosevelt's biographers, Edmund Morris, wrote about Marcus Hanna's achievement in industry and politics, stating, "He had not done badly in either field; he had made seven million dollars and a President of the United States." Marcus Hanna was perhaps one of the most influential political titans at the turn of the century. He alone developed the modern political campaign system in which a consistent message is delivered to the nation. Although conservative in many views, he was equally critical of the exploitative entrepreneurs and the radical practices of organized labor.

As Hanna was dying of typhoid, another fire just down the road from Washington, D.C., made headlines. This particular incident would prove again the inadequacies of America's public water utilities and the failure of addressing large-scale fires. The Great Baltimore Fire raged in Maryland from Sunday to Monday, February 7 and 8, 1904. Over 1,200 firefighters were called upon to bring the fire under control. One reason for the fire's duration was the lack of national standards in firefighting equipment. Fire engines from nearby cities such as Washington, D.C., and Philadelphia, along with units from New York City, Virginia, Wilmington and Atlantic City responded, but many could not help because their hose couplings could not fit Baltimore's hydrants. Much of the destroyed area was rebuilt in a relatively short period of time, and the City of Baltimore adopted a building code that stressed the use of fireproof materials. Perhaps the greatest legacy of the fire was the impetus it gave to efforts to standardize firefighting equipment in the United States, especially hose couplings.

Almost forgotten today is the fact that in past centuries, fires regularly swept through cities and frequently destroyed large areas. Close living quarters and unenforced or nonexistent building codes greatly contributed to both the frequency and the extent of city fires. The rapid growth of American cities in the nineteenth century contributed to the danger.

Firefighting practices and equipment were largely nonstandardized because each city had its own system. As time passed, these cities invested more in the systems they already had, increasing the cost of any conversion. Additionally, early equipment was often patented by its manufacturer. By 1903, there were over six hundred sizes and variations of fire hose couplings in the United States. Although efforts to establish standards had been made since the 1870s, there was very little progress because no city wanted to abandon its system. Few cities saw any reason to adopt standards, and equipment manufacturers did not care to compete with each other.

The first report of a fire that quickly spread was for the John Hurst and Company building in Baltimore on the morning of February 7. It quickly became apparent that the fire was far beyond the ability of the city's firefighting resources to fight, and calls for help were telegraphed to other cities. By early afternoon, units from Washington, D.C., had arrived. To halt the fire, officials decided to use a firebreak and dynamited buildings around the existing fire. This plan quickly proved to be inadequate, and it wasn't until 5:00 p.m. the next day that the fire was finally brought under control.

The fire's endurance was caused by more than just the lack of national standards in firefighting. Units from New York City were on the way but were blocked by a train accident, and they did not arrive until the next day. The crews brought their own equipment. High winds and winter freezing temperatures added to the difficulty for firefighters and further contributed to the severity of the fire. As a result, the fire burned over thirty hours, destroying 1,545 buildings that spanned seventy city blocks, a total of 140 acres.

While Baltimore was criticized for its hydrants, this was a problem that was not unique to Baltimore. It is unfortunate that it took a tragedy of this size before a stronger push was made to standardize municipal fire hydrants nationwide. This combined with other outbreaks of fire, floods and disease nationwide presented a grand opportunity for the City of Columbus to be progressive and innovative in solving a multifaceted problem. Columbus was about to demonstrate to the world how to correctly address the general welfare of the public as it applied to supplying, purifying and distributing water. Its comprehensive strategy would also help prevent the outbreak of waterborne disease epidemics by treating wastewater prior to returning it to a river that serviced other communities downstream.

CHAPTER TEN

Hanna's Death Played Out in the Columbus Press

A fter drifting in and out of consciousness for several days, Marcus Hanna died of typhoid fever on the evening of February 15, 1904, possibly from consuming tap water during a brief visit to Columbus during a typhoid epidemic in the city. The result of such headlines motivated the public to pass a bond issue in late 1904 to construct a water-supply dam and state-of-the-art potable water and wastewater treatment plant. Just ninety days prior to his death, Senator Hanna was at the top of his game, fame and power.

For the first week of his illness, the Senator was confined to his bed in his apartment in the Arlington Hotel. In Washington, D.C., on February 5, a statement was issued by his physicians that said Senator Hanna was officially diagnosed as having typhoid fever. Meanwhile, in Columbus, the news of Hanna's illness was made public with a simple *Columbus Dispatch* headline that read, "Senator Hanna Has Typhoid Fever." Each succeeding day, the *Dispatch* front page presented more news placing the origin of the senator's typhoid illness squarely on the Columbus water supply with statements such as, "Senator M.A. Hanna Drank Scioto Water When Here" and "Superintendent of Health, Dr. McKendree Smith, Believes the Senator Became Inoculated While Visiting in This City." This last article continued to report:

> [T]*yphoid fever has claimed the most noted man of the state for its victim, Senator*
> *M. A. Hanna. It is believed that to Columbus must be ascribed the responsibility*
> *for inoculating the great statesman with the disease germs. Dr. McKendree Smith,*

Hanna's Death Played Out in the Columbus Press

Superintendent of Ohio Health Department is firmly of the opinion that Senator Hanna's illness is directly traceable to his visit during the inauguration of Gov. Myron T. Herrick.

That statement initiated public accusations of blame toward the Columbus Water Works for Hanna's illness.

Dr. McKendree Smith became the band leader of the Hanna-typhoid-Columbus link once the newspaper printed a health officer's statement that read: "There is little doubt in my mind that Senator Hanna drank from the typhoid bearing water during his visit to Columbus upon the occasion of Gov. Herrick's induction into office. At that time the epidemic was just becoming fairly launched and the waters that circulated through the water system was contaminated from the State Hospital for the Insane."

Another headline, titled "Senator Drank Unboiled Water here" reported:

A sufficiently long period has elapsed to make this theory not only tenable but extremely probable. The Senator undoubtedly drank unboiled water, which may or may not have been filtered. In either case the result would have been the same since his system was in a condition for the reception of the bacilli and no filter yet designed will remove these minute organisms.

A few back-page stories shifted blame to the State of Ohio, though not as loudly as the front-page ones, which stated that no source had been traced.

The Senator was here at the time the infection from the tributary stream, Dry Run Creek[,] was still pouring into the Scioto and before the direct source of the pollution was traced to the fecal matter of the State Hospital for the Insane. So while Columbus and the Health Department deeply regrets the Senator's illness and is sincerely sorry that he should have taken into his system the disease germs while a guest of the Capital City, the State and not the City of Columbus, is responsible for his infection since the direct cause of this present epidemic is the State Hospital, a Buckeye Institution.

It was common in Columbus for some merchants and businessmen to take full advantage of a typhoid epidemic to market their service or product in the *Columbus Dispatch*. Since public knowledge of a typhoid fever epidemic generally starts with an announcement to boil water before use, the first establishments to exercise their bragging rights were the saloons and beer vendors. The common reasoning was that the adult public should be at ease drinking beer because it didn't require boiling. One such vendor was the local Hoster Brewing Company, which claimed specifically in a newspaper advertisement that drinking beer was better for your health. The boasted health benefits and the product's no-boiling-necessary tagline allowed the brewing company to more or less capitalize on public fear of consuming the public water supply. In many ways, this was merely an early way of calling the public's attention to a "fast food beverage." This was in contrast to the traditional teatime, which required some preparation versus just popping a bottle cap or cork.

Previously, the construction of the water-storage dam had been delayed because of political bickering and sideline agendas. But Marcus Hanna's death from typhoid removed all bottlenecks to the issue of building the dam. It was time to seriously address the root cause of the typhoid epidemic. The immediate result of Hanna's death was that the press would not let go of the tragedy that was caused by Columbus not critically addressing the need for a new water-storage dam and treatment plant in time to prevent the death of Hanna and other people whom the community held in high regard. The details of Hanna's rich life, career and contributions were paraded out to the public by the press for the next two weeks following his death.

The reporting of the private funeral train that transported Hanna's body from Washington, D.C., to Cleveland was reminiscent of President Abraham Lincoln's funeral train in 1865. The death of Hanna's friend President William McKinley had occurred just thirty-six months previously, and the two losses were closely associated. Large crowds assembled at the major stops and depots along the train's route to Cleveland as the funeral train was a sight to behold. The railroad entourage consisted of six coaches, a baggage car containing flowers, dining cars, two sleepers, a private car for the family and an observation car, in which rested the big black casket and an abundance of flowers.

On February 18, it was announced that federal office buildings in Ohio would not be open for business because President Roosevelt had issued the following order: "As a mark of respect in the memory of Honorable Marcus A. Hanna, late senator from the state of Ohio, it is hereby ordered that all federal offices in Ohio be closed during the hours of the funeral tomorrow, Friday, the nineteenth day of February."

On February 18, at 8:45 a.m., the Hannah funeral train pulled into Salem, Ohio, and stopped for ten minutes to take on Governor Herrick and his staff. Thousands of people were at the station standing in the winter cold to pay mute homage to the late illustrious senator.

Hanna's Death Played Out in the Columbus Press

At the railway station, additional members of Governor Herrick's staff boarded the funeral train. Once the members of his staff had joined him at Salem, Governor Herrick, on behalf of the State, extended to the bereaved family the condolence of all Ohio citizens. The place where this sad ritual was performed seemed fitting, for it was at Lisbon in Columbiana County, near Salem, that Senator Hanna was born and where he began his career. Once the train came to a stop at the Cleveland rail station, the first to leave it was Governor Herrick, followed by his staff. The chamber of commerce committee soon alighted, followed by members of the funeral party. Other members of the funeral party included Frank V. Bennetto, manager of the Arlington Hotel, in which the senator lived and died; Miss Morton of Philadelphia; one of the senator's nurses; and Congressman Charles Dick, his wife and several employees and servants. Dick would later be appointed to succeed Hanna in the U.S. Senate.

The funeral train arrived in Cleveland half an hour earlier than expected. The *Columbus Dispatch* reporting on the funeral events unfolding in Cleveland on February 18 stated the following:

> *All that remains mortal of the late Senator Marcus A. Hanna arrived in this his home city, today by way of the Pennsylvania Railroad. The air was charged with frost and heavy clouds filled with snow hung over the city. Snowstorms at various intervals made for a very gloomy day and in keeping with the gloom which had overcast Cleveland since the death of her most distinguished citizen. Not since the body of the martyred twentieth President James Garfield lay in state here has there been such deep and sincere grief.*

Hanna's coffin was placed beneath the canopy stands and catafalque that were used three years earlier as a platform for the remains of President McKinley during his Canton, Ohio services. As lifelong friends and companions, it was thought fitting that the same bier should be used for Senator Hanna that was in the funeral services for President McKinley. It was reported that the same flag that draped McKinley's casket was used to cover Hanna's coffin. The auditorium where the Senator's body lay in state was beautifully decorated with a wide variety of floral arrangements. Many handsome designs were placed about the room, and there was a profusion of small pieces and cut flowers. At the head of the bier stood an eight-foot-high pillar made up of lilies of the valley, violets and ferns. It had been sent by the staff of the Union National Bank, of which Marcus Hanna was the president.

Naturally, Marcus Hanna was not the only notable casualty of the Columbus epidemic. The Columbus press reported in detail that Charles Detterding, a young twenty-six-year-old pharmacist, died in the Protestant Hospital in Columbus following a three-week illness with typhoid. As a single man, he boarded at Mrs. Redmond's on Gift Street on the west side of Columbus and had been employed at a Gift Street Pharmacy since September 1903. Hanna and Detterding's death clearly show that typhoid was not a discriminating disease in regards to age or wealth.

One Columbus newspaper headline following Marcus Hanna's death read, "Typhoid Claims Director Wise." Specifically, the YMCA's physical director, Fred D. Wise, passed away in Grant Hospital at the age of thirty-two. He had been ill for three weeks with typhoid fever and had been expected to recover until he suffered a relapse. His condition grew steadily worse until, as stated in the vernacular of the times, "death placed its seal upon his eyes."

Another big headline in the *Columbus Dispatch* during this typhoid epidemic read, "Whisky Barrels Used in which Water is furnished to Schools." The article continued to point out that the barrel water was so tainted that the liquor was easily detectable on the children's breath. A big commotion between parents and the school board was escalating throughout the city because it was reported that the Crystal Ice Company was delivering water to the schools using recycled whisky barrels. (This is apparently how Crystal Ice was able to qualify at $1.40 a barrel as the low bidder for a contract to supply distilled water to school.) The school board awarded the contract because of the typhoid epidemic and the "boil water alert." The matter was expected to really heat up further because Mrs. Annie W. Clarke, who was the state president of the Ohio Women's Christian Temperance Union, was going to get to the bottom of this disturbing "kerfuffle" that threatened the spiritual integrity and innocence of young children.

These headlines, along with the report of Senator's Hanna's death, were the fuel used to boost the public's awareness that it was time for the community to be firm and push the point regarding the need for a new water supply in Columbus. In 1904, the Midwest, Columbus included, endured the greatest typhoid epidemic it had ever experienced.

CHAPTER ELEVEN
New Stars of the Twentieth Century

U p until the time of his death on January 18, 1937, John Gregory was one of the few engineers actively identified with the great advances made in the art of water purification and sewage treatment. Mr. Gregory was born in Cambridge, Massachusetts, on August 7, 1874, and graduated from MIT in 1895 with a bachelor's degree in civil engineering, having studied under Ellen Swallow Richards. He was employed in the design and construction of a number of waterworks projects that included the Water Filtration Plant in Albany, New York, the first large sand-filtration water facility built in the United States.

In January 1904, just prior to the news break about Marcus Hanna's illness, Gregory came to Columbus via an invitation by city engineer Julian Griggs and was employed by the City from that date through 1908, working as the engineer-of-design, and then the principal assistant engineer and engineer-in-charge. Griggs obtained $46,000 in funding for Gregory to design and build the initial sewage-testing station that became the first large-scale municipal sewage-testing station ever built, at which experiments were made on various methods of purifying sewage as well as on water softening. He was later in charge of both the design and construction of the Scioto River Water Purification and Softening Plant and the Columbus Sewage Treatment Plant. This potable water plant was the third largest rapid sand-filtration water treatment plant in the United States and, at that time, was the largest water softening facility ever constructed. This major project became known internationally as "The Columbus Experiment."

Left: In later years, Dr. John H. Gregory went on to become a professor of civil and sanitary engineering at Johns Hopkins University. His last project was the establishment of the Columbus Jackson Pike wastewater treatment plant in 1937. *FHJH.*

Below: Building a sewage testing station on the Scioto River was the first step in determining the nature and condition of the contaminated water prior to designing a comprehensive sewage treatment plant. *CDW.*

In 1908, Mr. Gregory returned to the East Coast, where he was employed as an engineer with the Metropolitan Sewage Commission of New York City. While there, he worked on investigations and studies pertaining to the collection, treatment and disposal of the sewage of the city of New York.

In 1911, he became a member of the firm of Hering and Gregory, Consulting Engineers and Sanitary Experts, in New York City. The firm's senior member was the late Rudolph Hering, one of the leading sanitary engineers of the country and often referred to as the dean of sanitary engineering in the United States. In 1918, Gregory was again employed by the City of Columbus to investigate and report on the water supply for the city. In his reports, Gregory recommended certain reinforcements to the waterworks distribution system, additions to the water purification and softening works and the construction of a storage dam and reservoir (later named the O'Shaughnessy Dam) on the Scioto River, to be located upstream from the Julian Griggs Dam. In 1920, Gregory was again retained by the City as a consulting engineer on these projects and served as such working with Clarence Hoover and Charles "Brownie" Cornell until 1925, the year the projects were substantially completed. In 1926, Gregory was called back again to Columbus as consultant on a significant sewage treatment problem, which had then become a major concern. This engagement involved consultation and advice on the design and construction of many miles of large sewer storm standby tanks on the Scioto River and Alum Creek and the new activated sludge sewage treatment works (Jackson Pike Wastewater Plant). Here again, it is of interest to note that the storm standby tanks were the first to be designed and placed under construction in the United States.

Gregory hired two brothers to assist him in managing this massive project: Clarence B. Hoover, who had charge of the wastewater operation, and Charles P. Hoover, who was the chemist in charge of the potable waterworks. The water treatment and softening plant and the sewage treatment works became known internationally as the Columbus Experiment, and engineers came from all over the world to watch the trickling system of sewage treatment, because it was regarded as the most economical to operate if it could be perfected in a freezing climate. The Hoovers helped to shape the water treatment industry and were committed to continuously improving treatment methods. Charles Hoover is credited with the co-discovery of a water softening process using lime and soda ash. Their efforts reduced the number of deaths resulting from typhoid in the early twentieth century.

Above: These filter-control consoles were built to last and remained in service for six decades. *CDW.*

Left: Clarence B. Hoover (1882 –1949), was hired by John Gregory in 1904 to operate the new sewage testing laboratory on the Scioto River south of downtown. He became the superintendent of water and wastewater after the death of Jerry O'Shaughnessy in 1921. *PC.*

Clarence B. Hoover (1882–1949) was an internationally known authority and pioneer in water purification and municipal water supply and brought Columbus worldwide recognition. His service with the City began in 1904 when he was employed at the old sewage-testing station on Moler Street before the sewage disposal plant was built. Hoover was a native of Ross, Ohio, and first came to Columbus in 1899. He attended Ohio State University, where he played left field on the Ohio State baseball squad. He graduated in 1903 with a degree in agriculture and special training in chemistry and bacteriology. During World War I, he served as captain of a utilities division at the army supply base at Norfolk, Virginia.

Charles P. Hoover (1884–1950) was born in Butler County, Ohio, and also moved to Columbus in 1899. He graduated from the Ohio State University in 1908 with a degree in chemistry. Immediately after graduation, he began working for the Columbus Water Works, first as a chemist and then chemist-in-charge and finally as superintendent of both water and sewage facilities. From the very beginning of his career as a chemist and engineer, Charles was concerned with the softening and purification of municipal and industrial water supplies. During his forty years in charge of the Columbus water softening and purification plant, he was completely absorbed with every detail of water treatment, constantly attempting to improve upon the original concepts of water treatment. His laboratory experiments and studies were numerous.

Dr. Charles P. Hoover (1884–1950) was appointed head chemist in charge of the new waterworks in 1908. Even today, his advanced work in water treatment continues to improve the quality of life for millions of people worldwide. *PC.*

The spotlight of the typhoid epidemic and Senator Hanna's death was not on Columbus alone. The State of Ohio, in the eyes of many, was also responsible because of the lax standards tolerated throughout the state in regards to drinking water. Between 1906 and 1907, another one of Ellen Swallow Richards's former students, Philip Burgess, started conducting a unique survey of water treatment plants in Ohio as a special engineer working for the State Board of Health.

Philip Burgess (1876–1972) was born in Newtonville, Massachusetts, and received his engineering degree in 1899 from MIT. In the course of performing the survey for the health board, Burgess collected 1,503 raw water samples for a comprehensive study that resulted in a 282-page report submitted to the state legislature. The report was the first clear depiction of the performance of Ohio's 27 water plants that had been built between 1895 and 1907 and established a standard for water quality. His work accelerated the understanding of the need to install purification plants where raw surface water was to be used as the domestic supply.

Before going into private practice, Burgess served as city engineer for Grandview Heights, Ohio. In 1912, Burgess started practicing general civil engineering and partnered with Chester Niple to establish the nationally renowned firm of Burgess and Niple. One of the earliest projects for the firm was the new purification works for the cities of Niles and Delaware, Ohio,

Philip Burgess (1876–1972) was a former MIT student of Ellen Swallow Richards and worked for the Ohio Health Department during the Columbus Experiment years, performing quality assessments on the other water plants in the state. He reported to the Ohio Legislature that a vast number of improvements in water treatment was needed in Ohio. *PC.*

Philip Burgess (far left) worked to upgrade the water and wastewater systems in other communities by using the lessons learned from the success of the Columbus Experiment. *PC.*

both of which employed one of the first rapid sand filtration systems ever built. Although Burgess was not involved with the Columbus Experiment, one of the most notable projects designed by Burgess and Niple was the Hoover Dam and Reservoir in Columbus. Philip Burgess was also a former chairman of the American Water Works Association, Ohio Section.

CHAPTER TWELVE

Land Acquisition and a New Dam

C onstruction of the new water storage dam began in late 1904. As provided by state law, the private farms and property on the existing bank of the Scioto River were acquired by imposing eminent domain. Since the vast majority of the property was sloped, rural agriculture property, most residents accepted the initial offer of compensation without argument. Many of the farms had not seen profitable times since before the Panic of 1893, which was the most serious economic depression the United States had ever experienced up until that time. But overall, the U.S. economy began to recover in 1897. After the election of McKinley and with confidence restored with the Klondike Gold Rush, the economy began a ten-year rapid growth spurt up until the Panic of 1907. It is then fair to say that the Columbus Experiment was started during a time of prosperity and nearly completed prior to the bottom falling out of the economy again. We must remember that the 1906 San Francisco earthquake contributed to market instability, due to a great deal of money going from New York to San Francisco to aid in reconstruction.

But Columbus citizens passed a bond issue and the construction of comprehensive water and wastewater utility began. The original fifty-two-foot high dam structure was cut to thirty feet because of the Johnstown Flood. But the design was such that the additional height could be added in later decades as the community needed to expand its water supply. The new waterworks on Dublin Road was going to be the world's first and largest combined purification and softening water plant. The new sewage plant

Land Acquisition and a New Dam

This high water river condition during construction of the storage dam was anticipated and did not cause any delay in the building schedule. *CDW.*

just south of the city on Frank Road was going to also be an innovative technical project in that it would be the first large-scale facility to incorporate sprinkling filters in a northern climate. It was the implementation of so many "innovative firsts" that prompted Gregory to label this huge endeavor the Columbus Experiment. Although most of the technology had been proven, it had not been applied in so great a magnitude.

The successful bidder for the storage dam construction project was local contractor James Westwater. The work of building a dam involves only a few major operations, but the extent of each was massive. It started with installing a railroad track spur, on which cars were left for loading excavation spoil material and unloading construction material and aggregate. A construction wench line spans the river and is supported by temporary timber towers. This was used to convey material (such as concrete) to any specific place along the dam when placing concrete. Workmen began excavating the site to place concrete for the formidable foundation. Next, the dam was built in the negative by placing wood forms made of lumber and posts that were flawless so far as knots. The reinforced steel rods were from a Cleveland mill and shipped by train. The construction of the dam involved a large-scale excavation of approximately thirteen thousand cubic yards of earth, the removal of thirty thousand cubic yards of rock and the placing of over fifty-seven thousand cubic yards of concrete.

Workmen dewatering and clearing a lower-level work site following a high water river condition. *CDW.*

Other materials and components made by specialty contractors to be installed as an integral part of the dam included steel gates and tunnel liners, waterstop material, joint-filling compounds to prohibit the movement of water, manual controls and valves. The thirty-foot dam was designed with the potential for subsequently retrofitting a hydroelectric power generator if the dam height was, by chance, raised an additional twenty-two feet, giving a total height of fifty-two feet for additional water storage.

Concrete was produced on site using cement and aggregate that was brought in by rail. Mixing cement and water causes a chemical reaction that hardens the concrete and releases heat. This distinct rise in the temperature inside a mass of concrete is of concern because, when the concrete begins to cool, it shrinks and cracks could result, potentially causing leaks. To limit these effects, workmen had to place the concrete when the air temperature was low. Furthermore, the concrete was placed in the forms only a few feet at a time and in narrow blocks. Then it was allowed to cure for at least seven days to allow the heat to dissipate.

The Scioto River Dam is a structure designed to store water for drinking and to supply power. The components of an overflow dam are designed so

The complete dam in 1905. The three round ports on the left were to be outlets for hydroelectric power in the future if the dam height were to be increased to fifty-two feet as originally designed. *CDW.*

This picture of the dam from the reservoir side shows the reinforced concrete forms in place for the west abutment. *CDW.*

that the water can be released and the level of the water in the reservoir regulated by a series of sluice gates, and a spillover outlet called a morning glory. Gregory designed a gravity dam with some curvature for additional strength, given the nature of the riverbed. The curved concrete structure is 1,006 feet in length, with the convex side up stream.

The reservoir is 5.8 miles long, with a surface area of 363 acres and a mean depth of 14.5 feet. The present capacity is 1.72 billion gallons, of which 1.49 billion gallons are available. If completed, the capacity of the 52.0-foot reservoir would be 5.45 billion gallons of raw water. The Scioto River above the reservoir has a drainage area of 1,032.0 miles.

Prior to construction, the water in the Scioto streambed was diverted to restrict the flow through the site. In this case, a cofferdam (a temporary structure to impound the water) was built to divert water into another area downstream from the dam site. The foundation area for the concrete dam had to be immaculately prepared prior to any concrete for the dam being placed. Since this dam was to be used primarily as a reservoir, it required a detailed process of excavating, cleaning and repairing the rock throughout the foundation "footprint" and on both abutments (the river bank sides that form the ends of the dam). The idea was to build the reservoir like a bowl, where it is equally sound around its perimeter.

Another shot of the Griggs Dam during when the river waters were high. *CDW.*

Land Acquisition and a New Dam

Aside from the use of a few steam-power machines, the storage dam was largely built by the strong backs of manual labor that was periodically supplemented with a mule team. Forms made of wood were constructed along the edges of each section of the dam. Steel reinforcement bars were placed inside the forms and tied to any adjacent rebar that was previously installed. The concrete was then poured. The height of each placed section of concrete is typically only five feet and the length and width of each dam section to be poured as a unit was only twenty-five feet. Construction continued in this way as the dam was raised section by section.

As soon as a significant portion of the dam was built, the process of filling the reservoir began. This was done in a highly controlled manner to evaluate the stresses on the dam and observe its early performance. A temporary emergency spillway was constructed because the work required more than one construction season. The upstream cofferdam was left in place as a temporary precaution, but it was not designed to hold more than minimal stream flows and rainfall and was dismantled as soon as it was practical.

The completion of the dam was celebrated with a formal christening ceremony and dedication on the afternoon of Tuesday, November 28, 1905. A contest was held to elect a Columbus schoolgirl to be the official "sponsor" for the structure, which was called the "Jeffrey Dam" at the

Robert Jeffrey (1876–1961) was president of the Columbus Board of Trade and was only twenty-nine years old when he was elected mayor of Columbus. The Columbus Experiment was initiated while he was in office. *CCJ.*

Although the thirty-foot-high storage dam was completed in 1905, this photo shows the fifty-two-foot high abutments that were designed to increase the height of the dam for additional water storage capacity. *CDW.*

time, after the existing mayor, Robert Jeffrey. The conditions of the contest stated that anyone could vote by just submitting a Columbus schoolgirl's name whose parents were from Columbus to the secretary of the board of trade. The successful candidate would be allowed to invite thirty friends as her guests and would be taken to the dedication in a private car. When the voting was complete one interesting name stood out. That name was Miss Mary Westwater, and she was the twelve-year-old daughter of the general contractor, James Westwater. Mary Westwater also took part in the dedication of Hoover Dam some fifty years later.

In 1905, Charles F. Kipp, a former reporter for the *Columbus Citizen* newspaper, was the first person to be appointed to the dam tender of the new storage dam. Kipp represented the *Columbus Citizen* at the formal dedication ceremonies. Columbus city engineer Julian Griggs appointed him the first "superintendent of the dam." As superintendent, Mr. Kipp was responsible for manually opening and closing the gates that controlled the flow of water through the dam. Additionally, he would act as river patrolman, perform weather forecasting and maintain records of area precipitation.

Kipp was born in Muskingum County, Ohio, in 1853. At the age of seventeen, he changed his name to Charles when his family moved to

Charles F. Kipp was the first superintendent of the storage dam. His duties included opening and closing the gates and valves of the dam and acting as one of the river patrolman. *PC.*

The City of Columbus provided this house to its first dam superintendent, Charles Kipp, and his family. *PC.*

Columbus. Upon arriving in Columbus by stagecoach from Zanesville, the Kipp family made their first home at Friend and Miller Streets (Friend Street was later changed to Main Street). His working career in Columbus began as a driver for a horse-drawn streetcar on the High Street Line. He later became superintendent of the State and Oak Street Line. In 1881, he was elected constable on the Democratic city ticket. And in 1890, he became a newspaper reporter for the *Columbus Press*. As the "government building reporter," he spent a lot of time at the old Columbus City Hall on State Street that was later destroyed by fire in 1921.

As superintendent of the new dam, Kipp was additionally compensated with the privilege of living rent-free in a large two-story frame home on city grounds just north of the dam. He lived in the home with his wife, Ruth Lewis Kipp, and their six children. Living at the dam was like having your own private park, according to one of his daughters, Alma Lu Kipp. She was sitting in a tree at the dam in late April 1906 when the news arrived about the San Francisco earthquake and the fires that resulted.

Charles Kipp, Julian Griggs and Jerry O'Shaughnessy resigned their public service positions in 1908 due to a change in city administration. The following year, Kipp bought an interest in a newspaper in Muskogee, Oklahoma. He died three year later on March 10, 1911.

CHAPTER THIRTEEN
Water and Equipment

The new waterworks on Dublin Road, located about one mile from the State Capitol building, was a masterpiece of engineering technology. Like the storage dam, the construction of the purification plant used a few steam-powered machines. But it was largely built with manual labor, and many of these men were very highly skilled. The construction trades in Columbus at that time were integrated with whites, blacks and any variety of foreign nationals who didn't speak English. Materials were site delivered by railroad car and by mule-drawn wagon teams. The original plant was a series of buildings arranged in a way that maximized the efficiency of the purification process as the raw water flowed through the various stages of treatment.

The river water flowed a distance of 4.3 miles from the storage dam, downstream to the intake dam, the site of the old Jaeger dam near West Spring Street. At this point, a usable amount of raw river water entered a small masonry structure with a slate roof called the intake screen house. This was the first step of treatment, where the sticks, leaves and even fish and snails were removed as they were caught by a screen chamber and returned to the river.

From there, the raw water would flow through a conduit by gravity to the Scioto River Pumping Station, located on the north bank of the river about one mile upstream of the confluence of the Scioto and the Olentangy River. The pumping equipment consisted primarily of two twenty-six-inch Worthington volute centrifugal pumps driven by Harrisburg tandem four-valve engines. These are referred to as low service pumps and are used to

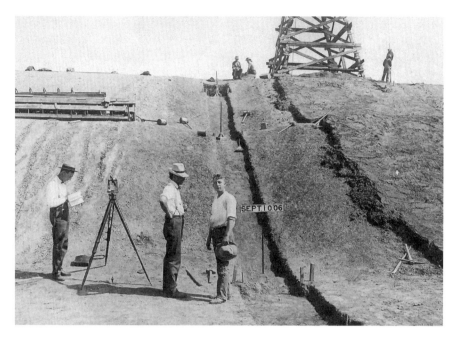

A survey crew laying out the line boundaries and grade of the settling basins. *CDW.*

Workmen using the overhead conveyor line bucket to place concrete in the forms for the clearwell roof deck. *CDW.*

The raw water (river water) intake house. This is the only structure still standing today and is in excellent condition. *CDW.*

push the water through the various cycles of purification processing. In addition, there were the high-service pumps, which consist of two Holly Vertical Triple Expansion steam-pumping engines that were used to pump the finished water from the filtered water clearwell (reservoir) into the distribution system. The pump station was also equipped with two one hundred-kilowatt, steam-driven direct-current generators, four three-hundred-horsepower Babcock and Wilcox coal-fired boilers, wash water pumps, a condenser, flush pumps and various feed pumps. Coal and other bulk supplies and chemicals were primarily delivered by railcar off a special rail spur that was built to convey freight directly to the pump station and the chemical storage head house.

The Holly engines of the Scioto River Pumping Station were a fabulous work of mechanical art and served the public faithfully for sixty-one consecutive years. They were manufactured and tested in Lockport, New York, where they were then dismantled and the components placed on a canal boat and sent down the Ohio Erie Canal to Columbus. Once they reached Columbus, the components were unloaded on to a flatbed railcar

The three-hundred-horsepower boilers used to produce the steam for the Holly engines were custom built on-site at the Scioto River Pumping Station specifically for that application. *CDW.*

and transported to the construction site. The Holly Triple Expansion Engine was a compound steam engine. It operated through three stages of cylinders, each with a different pressure level, and it was regarded as the state-of-the-art method of improving energy efficiency. Up until the development of compound engines, steam engines used the steam only once before recycling it back to the boiler, but a compound engine recycles the steam into one or more larger, lower-pressure second cylinders first, in order to utilize more of its heat energy. Originally developed as maritime technology, the compound engines could be configured to increase either a ship's economy or its speed.

American engineer James P. Allaire installed the first compound engine in a ship, the *Henry Eckford*, in 1824. However, many sources attribute the "invention" of a maritime compound engine to Glasgow's John Elder in the 1850s. Elder made improvements to the compound engine, which made it safe and economical for ocean-crossing voyages for the first time.

Prior to and during World War I, expansion steam engine technology dominated marine applications where high vessel speed was not essential. The manufacturing of multiple-expansion engines continued well into

Water and Equipment

The main smokestack of the Scioto River Pumping Station was a 140-foot-tall brick masonry structure built by local Columbus brickmasons. *CDW.*

the twentieth century. All 2,700 Liberty ships built by the United States during World War II were powered by triple-expansion engines, because the capacity of the U.S. to manufacture steam turbines and diesels was still limited. The biggest manufacturer of triple expansion engines during the war was the Joshua Hendy Iron Works. Henry J. Kaiser also had a major role in the Joshua Hendy Iron Works in California, which built the EC-2 Triple Expansion Steam Engines for the Liberty ships.

The Columbus Experiment Water Purification Works was designed for softening and filtering the river water, and on account of the extremely variable characteristics of the untreated water, ample flexibility was sought in its operation. There was a storage house for chemicals and a head house, which stores the equipment for making and feeding the lime, soda ash and coagulant solutions. This building also housed the chemical and bacteriological laboratories and Mr. Charles Hoover's office.

The coagulant solution involved alum that had been made using a unique alum plant devised by Mr. Hoover. The compact alum plant was the first

Above: Aerial view of the washwater tank. The tank holds clean water used to clean the sand filters of the water treatment plant. *CDW.*

Left: Interior view of the headhouse looking at the bulk chemical conveyor system. *CDW.*

of its kind ever built at a purification works. The small in-house processing facility could produce between eight hundred and one thousand tons of alum annually. The process of making the aluminum sulfate syrup began by jointly heating bauxite (a high aluminum clay that was delivered by railroad freight car) and sulfuric acid and applying the final solution to the raw water. The insoluble silica present in the alum syrup mixes with the mud in the raw water and congeals into larger flocculent particles that sink to the bottom of a settling basin as sediment and are removed.

The plant layout included a lime saturator composed of six twenty-five-feet square tanks, in which the lime is dissolved and the reaction or slaking process begins. There were two baffled reaction tanks (each two hundred feet long, twenty-five feet wide and twenty feet deep) and a settling basin that was divided into six compartments with a total capacity of fifteen million gallons. In these compartments, the greater part of the turbidity (suspended solids) and the precipitated materials are removed by sedimentation.

The innovative treatment plant had a separate filter house building that contained ten mechanical filter units. Each filter unit had a net filtering area of 1,089 square feet and, taken as a whole, had a rated capacity of 30 millions gallons per twenty-four hours. The finished filtered water was then conveyed to a covered filtered water reservoir called a clearwell that had

Settling basins and the headhouse where the bulk chemicals were stored and prepared for use in the various treatment processes. *CDW.*

The nearly completed Scioto River Pumping Station with the elevated rail spur and washwater tank on the left. *CDW.*

The flocculation tank room where the submerged mixing paddles were driven by belts from a central overhead line shaft. *CDW.*

The valve house corridor of the treatment basins was where the plant operators controlled the flow of water through the basins and various stages of treatment. *CDW.*

View of the pipe gallery located just below the filter building control console deck. *CDW.*

The underground clearwell held the finished drinking water before it was pumped to the community. *CDW.*

The curved and contoured concrete walls of the clearwell interior were an advanced engineering and construction work of art even by today's standards. *CDW.*

two compartments. In 1908, the total net capacity of the clearwell was 10 million gallons.

Once the water was treated, the distribution of the water to Columbus was accomplished by the high-service Holly engines pumping the finished product into two 36.0-inch cast-iron water mains that extended from the Scioto River Pumping Station to the west side stations, where they are cross-connected into the two 24.0-inch and one 20.0-inch mains that ran to the east and north districts of the city. The entire distribution system consists of over 260 miles of cast-iron pipe, of which 69 percent was 6 inches in diameter or smaller. A considerable length of 1.1-inch and 2.0-inch wrought-iron pipe was in use also and, as of 1908, practically the entire original piping was still in use.

The first water was pumped into the new thirty-millions-gallon-a-day water treatment plant from the storage dam on July 2, 1908. On August 17, the first water was pumped to consumers, while two days later, regular filtration and pumping were started. General water softening began on August 22, 1908. During the first six months the new waterworks was in operation, there were only six typhoid deaths. It took until 1919 to reduce

In addition to the water storage dam and treatment plant, new cast-iron water mains and valves had to be laid in order to properly serve the community. *CDW.*

Above: Aerial view of the Scioto River Pumping Station and combined treatment and softening plant. *CDW.*

Below: The completed 1908 Columbus Experiment Scioto River Pumping Station housed two 20 million gallons of water a day. Holly triple-expansion pumping engines conveyed the filtered and softened drinking water to the Columbus community. *CDW.*

the toll to one death and until 1940 to wipe the record clean: no cases, no deaths. Following one year of operation, Gregory hailed the combined filtration and softening works a success. The Columbus Experiment was the moon landing of its day, and it elevated John Gregory and the Hoover brothers to international fame.

CHAPTER FOURTEEN

Wastewater Plant

In 1905, construction of the Scioto River storage dam, along with the world's first combined purification and softening waterworks on Dublin Road, were finally underway. It was also at this time that the city engineer Julian Griggs proposed and obtained funding for a revolutionary new sewage treatment works that was designed by John H. Gregory. This project was to be located on the Scioto River, south of the city near Frank Road. The plant was an innovative application that employed the trickle-sprinkling filter system for the first time in a freeze-thaw northern climate.

But looking back over the twenty-five years prior to the Columbus Experiment, we see a rather unconventional history associated with the city's handling of sewage and wastewater. Starting in 1880, the cause of the long-feared mystery illness at the Ohio State Capitol building that was known as "Statehouse Malaria" was finally revealed. It was discovered that an inept contractor had connected all of the restroom toilets to the ventilating flues and not to the sewer systems. This mistake had been having an ill effect on all who entered the building since it was first occupied in 1861 at the start of the Civil War. The remediation involved workers shoveling twenty years of accumulated dried human waste into over 150 barrels for immediate removal. Once the appropriate sewer attachments were made, the mysterious illnesses were completely eliminated.

The population of Columbus had grown to 52,000 by 1880. Water service was supplying approximately 2.2 million gallons per day, with the majority of the water simply returning to the river and various streams through approximately 23.5 miles of sewer pipes and open ditches.

This photo shows the innovative trickle-spray system that the design engineer John Gregory incorporated into the new sewage treatment process. This had never been tried under cold weather climate conditions. *CDW.*

By 1890, Columbus had grown to a population of over 88,000 people, and as a result, the water and sewer line infrastructure was continually being expanded. Water usage had climbed to an average daily usage of 7 million gallons a day, with the majority returning to the Scioto River, the Olentangy River and Alum Creek through over seventy-eight miles of sewer lines. These sewer lines conveyed both wastewater and storm water runoff to various discharge points throughout the city along the two rivers and Alum Creek. It was estimated that approximately 90 percent of the sewer service area was being discharged into the Olentangy and Scioto Rivers. With the marked increase in growth and associated wastewater discharges, records indicated that the pollution in the Scioto River was becoming increasingly intolerable to the public, especially during the dry summer months and the periods of low river flows in the early fall.

Then, in 1892, the construction of an intercepting sewer was completed. This system picked up the numerous sewage discharge points and conveyed this effluent to a common outfall located below the central

The downtown banks of the Scioto River were often compromised with contaminated rain water and industrial pollution. *OHS.*

city. Although this did the job of eliminating the awful stench in the downtown area, the conditions just south of downtown had deteriorated to the point that an outraged public brought the matter to the attention of the State Board of Health.

City engineer Julian Griggs submitted a report in 1898 to the city council detailing the need for an improved wastewater treatment system. In addition to updating the collection system's network of pipes, Griggs proposed that a sewage treatment plant be constructed, one that would employ a mechanical screening system and double filtration at a rate of 500,000 gallons per acre a day, with a total sewage treatment capacity of 20,000,000 gallons a day. Griggs specifically advised that a scaled-down version of two acres be built and placed in service for a full season to confirm the validity of the design prior to fully developing the remaining thirty-eight-acre scheme. The report was based on investigations by Griggs and the engineer John W. Alvord and attempted to assess solutions to the local needs in the context of the best English and American practices in regard to sewage treatment and disposal. A second report by Griggs and a supplementary report by the esteemed engineer Rudolph Hering were presented in 1901.

By 1900, 80 percent of the city's population was being serviced by over 144 miles of public sewer. Since this was a combined sewer system that conveyed both untreated sewage and collected storm water to outlets at Alum Creek and the Scioto River, it had become an unpleasant public nuisance. The population had surpassed 125,000. The city leadership appointed a sewer commission and assigned Julian Griggs to be the first sewer commission engineer. Referring to Griggs' 1898 report, the commission recommended a capital improvement project to construct a state-of-the-art sewage treatment plant. The commission also offered a multiple septic tank holding system to provide about twelve hours of detention time as a lower-cost alternative. Various bond issues to finance construction were pursued. Luckily in 1901, the health board rejected the commission's lower-cost alternative as inadequate to serve the community's needs during low river flow. Shortly thereafter, the city's director of public improvements retained the services of a consulting engineer to review and advise the city with reference to "the whole sewage problem." The engineer, Rudolph Hering, submitted a report recommending the improvements originally proposed by Griggs, which specifically included additional sewer pipelines, a pumping station and a force-main and treatment plant consisting of large septic tanks and intermittent sand filters. The report further recommended "that the filters were not to be operated during those periods of relatively high water when the sewage could be disposed of on the basis of four cubic feet per second per 1,000 population." He also advised the City to conduct a pilot study of the proposed treatment works to determine the advisability of building the full-size plant using septic tanks or settling basins. The Ohio Board of Health approved the proposed plan on July 2, 1901, although there were reservations regarding the feasibility of septic tanks because of the local soil conditions. In November 1903, a bond issue was put before the public for a vote and was approved.

The Columbus sewage treatment plant basins were the most advanced in the modern world of 1908. *CDW.*

In 1904–05, an experimental sewage purification plant and testing station was constructed and operated under the direction of Rudolph Hering and George W. Fuller, consulting engineers for the City of Columbus. The results obtained here would determine the process to be adopted for the new sewage disposal system. The test station was located near the main sewage district discharge point to evaluate intermittent sand filters, as well as coke strainers, contact filters, septic treatment, chemical precipitation, plain sedimentation and sprinkling filters. Many of these systems had previously been proven to work effectively in several applications instituted by the British. At this time, sprinkling-filter technology had no record of ever being fully tested in a cold climate and under severe winter conditions. The questions about the viability of sprinkling filters in the Columbus project gave rise to the effort being looked upon as an experiment.

Recommendations from the evaluation presented in the *Report on Sewage Purification*, dated November 10, 1905, were as follows:

1. Preliminary clarification of the sewage in basins holding on an average about an eight-hour flow operated on the basis of the septic treatment.
2. Purification of the septic effluent to a nonputrescible state by sprinkling filters at an average net rate of two million gallons per acre daily.
3. Final clarification of the effluent of the sprinkling filters in basins holding an average flow of about two hours.

The report concluded, "This process produces a nonputrescible effluent of satisfactory appearance and from which about 90 percent of the bacteria in the raw sewage are removed."

The John H. Gregory papers describe the full wastewater and water program in great detail, credit the outstanding work of the sanitary engineering visionaries (including premiere figures of both national and local reputation in chemistry, plant operations and engineering who participated in the program) and contain a technical discussion of the program by twenty-five such luminaries. Among the discussion and comments were the remarks of Allen Hazen, who had done consulting work on the hydraulics of the Columbus program. Hazen had been a founder of Hazen & Whipple, ancestor firm of today's Malcolm Pirnie, Inc. He developed many of the basic methods of sanitary engineering, including what is known as the "Hazen-Williams Formula," which properly describes the flow of water in pipes.

Construction began immediately on the new treatment works located approximately two miles south of the existing outfall. Flow was delivered to the new treatment works through a thirty-six-inch force main from the Main Sewage Pumping Station. This station, although larger, was similar to the East Side Sewage Pumping Station, and was equipped with a sand catcher to remove gritty material and bar screens with one-inch openings in front and a half-inch in the rear to protect the centrifugal pumping equipment. Although the East Side Sewage Pumping Station used natural gas combustion engines to drive the pumps, those at the main pumping station were originally driven by steam. The total wastewater and water improvements needs of Columbus at the time were addressed in a combined program of contracts, which were the largest, most expensive public works undertaken in the history of the city. By the end of 1908, construction of the Improved Sewage Works, considered the City's first wastewater treatment plant, was completed and placed into service. The plant was designed to treat 20 million gallons a day, with a maximum hydraulic capacity of 45 million gallons a day. It consisted of septic tanks, followed by stone-filled "sprinkling filters" and settling tanks. The sprinkling filters, an attached-growth configuration of aerobic biological treatment, would be a precursor of later "trickling filters" (attached-growth biological treatment systems). The city's population was now 170,000, and 270 miles of sewer existed.

The Improved Water and Sewage Works went into service in the fall of 1908, and the same statistics showed only five total deaths from typhoid for the first six months of 1909. It was thought wise to provide a single purification plant in designing the system, to which the sewage from all parts of the city should be conducted for treatment. The East Side Sewage Pumping Station was provided to lift the sewage from Alum Creek Sewer District over the ridge into the East Side Intercepting Sewer District. The intercepting sewer was extended across the Scioto River and the sanitary and storm water systems on the city's west side were extended to the same point. The combined sewage of the city was then relayed by the Main Sewage Pumping Station through a forty-inch main to the Sewage Purification Works, about a mile below. The work also required about two and a half miles of levee construction, a railroad spur nearly two miles long and a single-track railroad bridge across the Scioto River.

The cost of the entire construction, including engineering and the purchase of 358 acres of land, was $1,351,020 and included the following:

EAST SIDE SEWAGE PUMPING STATION: The dry-flow sewage of the Alum Creek Sewer District was collected in the back of a low dam across the nine-foot Main Street sewer, about four hundred feet west of Alum Creek.

The East Side Sewage Pumping Station was designed to resemble a typical modest residential home. *CDW.*

From there it was then conducted through a 24-inch pipe to a sand catcher and then through coarse cage screens to the suction well. It was discharged through a 20-inch main over the ridge into the Mound Street sewer at Luckhaupt Avenue. The pump station was equipped with two 10-inch Worthington volute pumps, each driven through a Morse chain by a 16¼-inch by 20-inch Columbus single-cylinder horizontal engine that operates on natural gas. At that rate of discharge, averaging two million gallons per day, the total combined suction and discharge head on the pumps was fifty-eight feet.

MAIN SEWAGE PUMPING STATION: This station was built on the west bank of the Scioto River, two and a half miles south of the State House. In regular service, its orifice would lift the sewage of the entire city to the Purification Works, one and one-fourth miles below, but during periods of high water, the east side's sewage was discharged by gravity to the river while the capacity of the pumping equipment is devoted to the clearing of the low land on the west side.

The equipment comprises three twenty-inch and two twelve-inch Worthington volute pumps that are connected to Reeves vertical,

The architectural design and style of the Main Sewage Pumping Station was regarded as a very pleasant-looking industrial building despite its purpose. *CDW.*

cross-compound, condensing engines, two ten-kilowatt steam-driven generating sets, three 150-horsepower Babcock and Wilcox boilers, steam-operated screen cages and surface condensers. The pumping units deliver sewage to the Purification Works against an average total head of twenty-five feet.

During "low water, warm weather" conditions (from late spring until early fall), the flow in the Scioto River varies from twenty to thirty million gallons per day. A stream of this size was able to consume about one million gallons of normal Columbus dry-flow sewage per day without showing the evidences of gross pollution (which are offensive to both sight and smell). The dry-flow sewage of this city varies from fifteen to eighteen million gallons per day. If all of this sewage were discharged into the river without treatment, the river would be called upon to dispose of fifteen times more sewage than it was capable of consuming, and the results would be the conversion of the river into a large open sewer, which would be undesirable from both a sanitary and aesthetic point of view.

The problem of sewage treatment for this city may then be defined as follows: the treatment of the raw sewage should be carried to such an extent that the river, which is able to consume but one million gallons per day of partly purified sewage without showing the evidences of gross pollution, will remain viable.

The treatment of the sewage consists in preliminary sedimentation and clarification in large open concrete tanks, aeration and oxidation in sprinkling filters and final sedimentation and clarification in open, shallow concrete basins preceding the discharge of the treated liquid into the river.

All of the sewage of the city east of the Scioto River was collected by an intercepting sewer, which had its origin just north of Hudson Road near the Olentangy River and which roughly followed the Olentangy to its mouth before following the Scioto to a point about three thousand feet south of Greenlawn Avenue. This was where it crossed under the river and discharged into the suction wells of the Main Sewage Pumping Station. The intercepting sewer was almost seven miles in length, had an average grade of 0.1063 percent and received domestic and storm water sewage

Workman operating a steam-actuated gate hoist used to lift bar screens at the Main Sewage Pumping Station. *CDW.*

and trade wastes. A part of the sewage collected by the intercepting sewer was sewage from the Alum Creek Sewerage District, which had comprised that part of the city and naturally drained into Alum Creek. This sewage, after being collected by the network of sewers of this district, discharged into an outfall sewer (it formerly discharged into Alum Creek, but the creek would now conduct the sewage to the East Side Sewage Pumping Station). From the East Side Station, the sewage was pumped through a twenty-inch cast-iron force main that was 8,180 feet in length and into a gravity-flow sewer that then carried it to the intercepting sewer. The sewage of the city's west side was conducted to the Main Sewage Pumping Station through a large trunk sewer.

All of the sewage of the city, after reaching the Main Pumping Station, passed through coarse screens, which removed only the coarsest material such as rags, sticks, cans and paper. After being thoroughly screened, the sewage was pumped through a forty-eight-inch cast-iron force main (1.2 miles in length) to the Purification Works, where it discharged into open concrete tanks. These tanks were twelve feet deep and had a combined capacity of eight million gallons. Moreover, the tanks covered an area 423 feet long by 236 feet wide, and each tank was divided into six separate compartments. Any two or more of these compartments could be used together. From what has just been said regarding the collection of the sewage, it is evident that grades of the sewers and the distances through which the sewage traveled, resulted in the delivery of a stale sewage, which made rapid handling at the Purification Works desirable.

The sewage received at the Purification Works was a mixture of domestic and storm sewage and trade wastes and, consequently, carried, in suspension or solution, materials that are common to kitchen, lavatory, storm water and street drainage and wastes from various manufacturing concerns.

The total cost of the Columbus Experiment water and sewage improvements—including land acquisition and engineering—was $3,312,820. In today's dollars, the price tag would exceed $81,000,000. If the project had to be accomplished in the wake of today's safety and environmental regulations, it is estimated that the cost would conservatively exceed $265,000,000.

CHAPTER FIFTEEN

Results and Operation

By 1909, the new waterworks was being hailed as a success throughout the engineering community for its effectiveness, earning a five-star rating and boosting the reputations of virtually everyone associated with its creation. The outbreak of typhoid was drastically reduced by the dual stage treatment and softening process. But the threat of typhoid had still not been completely eradicated.

Before the Columbus Experiment, the river patrol force had seven men engaged in patrolling the banks of the Scioto and Olentangy Rivers and Alum Creek. In January 1910, the patrol staff was reduced by dropping the four least efficient men. Charles Hoover, the head chemist of water treatment operations, had two of the river patrolmen on his staff. The job of Mr. Evans and Mr. Burnside was to identify any possible sources of contamination along the Scioto River upstream from the plant intake. Far too often, the source was found to be a privy or outhouse located in close proximity to a tributary stream feeding into the river. Many outhouses were designed and built to discharge the human waste directly into the river. These unsanitary structures posed a substantial threat to the water supply of Ohio's capital city.

Because of the increasing population on the upstream watershed, preventive measure was as important as a cure for waterborne diseases in maintaining and protecting the water supply. With their other duties, these officers investigated all cases of infectious diseases on the watershed within twenty miles of the city, provided disinfectants and assisted in preventing

The Great Columbus Experiment of 1908

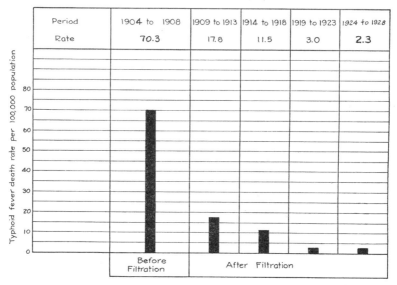

TYPHOID FEVER DEATH RATE BEFORE AND AFTER THE FILTRATION OF THE PUBLIC WATER SUPPLY

DIVISION OF WATER - COLUMBUS, OHIO

Period	1904 to 1908	1909 to 1913	1914 to 1918	1919 to 1923	1924 to 1928
Rate	70.3	17.8	11.5	3.0	2.3

Typhoid fever death rate per 100,000 population

Before Filtration — After Filtration

This chart shows the drastic reduction in typhoid outbreaks after the new water treatment technology was put into service. *CDW.*

This outhouse was declared a health hazard in 1911 by a river patrolman who said it was too close to the tributary stream, which can be seen in the background. *PC.*

pollution of the river. A watch was kept over the operation of several sewage disposal plants on the watershed, as well as on the many isolated sources of pollution. Largely through the efforts of the Columbus Water Division, smaller villages along the Scioto, such as Marble Cliff and Grandview Heights, made suitable provisions for the treatment of their own sewage.

Of particular concern to Charles Hoover was the potential spread of typhoid bacteria. In 1911, as a result of the international acclaim of the Columbus Experiment, Hoover was working with Theodore Thompson, head of the British government's health ministry, and Alexander Houston, director of the Metropolitan Water Board of London, England. Their research had confirmed that a typhoid carrier can carry the infection in his or her body and transmit it through exposure of stools or urine, even if the person is not exhibiting symptoms of the disease. Therefore, the bacterium could easily enter the water supply and the water treatment plant from the privy or outhouse along the river. We must keep in mind that the use of chlorine as a common disinfectant was still more than a decade away.

In a letter that was dated November 9, 1911, and sent to Walter W. Jackson, superintendent of the waterworks, Hoover explained that Columbus' more

Pictured here is a young Charles P. Hoover (far right), the newly appointed head chemist in charge of all water treatment operations, and his assistant (left) in the operations laboratory. This photo was taken in the summer of 1908. *CDW.*

impoverished population lived between the Scioto River Filtration Plant and the water-supply storage dam (Griggs Dam). Specifically, the letter addressed the hog wallows and livestock barnyards that sat on the tributaries leading to the Scioto River. Hoover also noted that endoparasitic (parasites that live in the internal organs of the host) diseases were more common than had been previously supposed. And since diseased hogs and cattle are the chief agencies of this type of infection, river water contaminated by other wildlife excrement may also contain the eggs and larvae of endoparasites. Hoover made it a point to emphasize that until more was known about the role of bacteria present in the excrement of hogs suffering from intestinal disorders, every precaution should be taken to prevent this source of pollution.

Charles Hoover, at age twenty-seven, was very serious about his role in preventing epidemics of typhoid or any other waterborne disease from plaguing Columbus or anywhere else in the world. Hoover was often called upon internationally to consult and share his insight regarding the advancement of water treatment as a science.

In April 1912, the largest volcanic eruption of the twentieth century occurred on Mount Katmai, and a new volcano called Novarupta formed as a result. The initial eruption actually took place at the Novarupta Volcano. During the eruption, the withdrawal of magma beneath Katmai resulted in the collapse of its summit area and formed a 2,000-foot-deep caldera. The 60-hour-long eruption expelled 3.1–3.6 cubic miles of magma, thirty-times as much as Mount St. Helens in Washington State produced when it erupted in 1980. Additionally, the eruption resulted in over 4.1 cubic miles of air fall and approximately 2.6 cubic miles of ash flow, and it ended with the extrusion of a lava dome that plugged the vent. The 295-foot high, 1,180-foot wide dome and the caldera it created formed the Novarupta Volcano.

During the fifth year of operations at the new Columbus Water Works on the Scioto River, an event occurred that put the plant out of service (the only time in the history of the Columbus Water Division that such has ever happened). The cause was due to high water resulting from a massive flood that hit a sizable portion of America's Midwest. The 1913 flood has been attributed in part to the 1912 eruption of Novarupta and the elder volcano Mount Katmai. In one of the greatest recorded volcanic events, Novarupta emitted such a tremendous amount of fine ash material into the atmosphere that it effectively reduced the earth's sunlight exposure and brought about a cooler climate over the Northern Hemisphere the following winter.

The March 1913 flood was created by a series of three winter storms that hit the Midwest region. Within three days, eight to eleven inches of rain

The March 1913 floodwaters and debris buildup on Neil Avenue next to the Ohio Penitentiary. *OHS.*

fell on the frozen ground of Central Ohio. The falling rain immediately turned into surface runoff that caused the Scioto River and its tributaries to overflow. Every low-lying flood plain in the state suffered. In Dayton, the levees failed, and the prosperous downtown area experienced floodwater as deep as nineteen to twenty feet. In Zanesville, the "Y" Bridge was washed out. (Zanesville was hit a second time by flooding that year in October.) But in Columbus, amid the actual chaos of the flooding in the Franklinton area, a very curious thing happened.

A frenzy of panic and terror filled Columbus about 4:30 p.m. Wednesday, March 26, 1913, as a rumor began to spread that the Scioto River storage dam had failed due to the flooding and burst open. At anytime, a huge body of water would sweep down on downtown Columbus. The rumor was passed around by word of mouth and by the telephone until all members of the community feared for their lives.

Franklinton, which is on the west side of the Scioto River, was already underwater from a gigantic flood that had killed over one hundred people just days before. The press had reported that dead bodies were lodged in trees and cemetery coffins were unearthed and detailed descriptions of all sorts of flood horrors over the previous forty-eight hours. The prospect of a wall of water rushing down the swollen river struck fear in the general population of downtown Columbus just across the river from the devastation and where people were, for the most part, unaffected by the flood. But once the rumor took hold, thousands of people believed that it was the end of the world. Stores in the downtown area were completely deserted, and people were fainting from fear and exhaustion. Hundreds ran to the dome of the State Capitol building and jammed the steps to the cupola in search of a higher perch for safety. Police and militiamen rushed into stores and office buildings, spreading the unfounded warning and adding to the confusion and terrific fear that had completely captured the downtown area. Thousands of men and women, young and old, professional and tradespeople took to the streets on foot and started running. Women were trying desperately to lead their sobbing children to safety as both stumbled, so paralyzed were they with fear. Horses released from stables ran through downtown, adding more confusion to the tumultuous crowd of people, vehicles, wagons and assorted domestic animals.

When no water rushed in, people gradually determined it was a false alarm. Columbus-born humorist James Thurber used the incident as the basis for his 1933 short story "The Day the Dam Broke." Thurber wrote: "Order was restored and fear dispelled by means of militiamen riding about in motor lorries (cars) bawling through megaphones, The Dam has not Broken!"

Next day's newspaper reported that if the dam had completely failed (according to Charles Hoover's calculations), it would have only added an extra two inches to the actual flood waters. City engineer Julian Griggs and James Westwater, the general contractor who constructed the dam, were both quoted in the newspaper the following day as stating, "The dam cannot break, and if it did it would not cause any additional damage." Unlike the Johnstown dam, which was an earthen dam, the Scioto storage dam was made of steel-reinforced concrete and anchored in a trench made of solid stone that was six to eight feet deep. During the high water mark of the flood, the water was nearly twelve feet above the crest of the dam. Additionally, the abutment ends were fifty-two feet high because the dam was designed and constructed to subsequently have an additional twenty feet in height added to increase city's supply of raw river water. At no time was there any danger of a dam failure. Apparently, the design engineers had designed the dam with the tragedy of the Johnstown Flood in mind, showing they had learned a lesson from past events.

During the early years of the new sewage plant's operation, it became evident that the preliminary septic tanks were inadequate and needed to be updated to assure good solids separation during extreme dry-weather, sanitary flow conditions. The grade of the sewers and long residence times of the wastewater in the collection system would "result in the delivery of a stale sewage." The City chose to modify the basins to conform to the "Emscher System," introduced by Dr. Imhoff. A small testing tank holding approximately 35,000 gallons was constructed in 1910 and put into operation in 1911. Success of this tank led to the construction of full-size Imhoff modifications to the existing septic tanks. Between 1910 and 1915, other infrastructure improvements were undertaken, including replacing natural gas and steam-powered prime movers for both pump stations with electric motors. In spite of the recent improvements, Columbus was "behind the eight ball." According to the City's 1915 annual report, "The severity of the problem at Columbus may be realized from the statement, previously made, that 20 million gallons of sewage are discharged into a stream whose discharge sometimes reaches a minimum of five MGD." The population had grown to 181,000 by 1915, and water consumption was in excess of 15 million gallons a day. Additionally, the sewer pipeline infrastructure had increased to 277 miles.

By 1917, work on the installation of the new Imhoff Tanks had finished. "There is entirely too much pollution of the stream above the treatment works," the City's annual report recorded that year. "This pollution should be stopped and we recommend that this be brought to the attention of the proper city, township, or county officials." In addition, the report for the Sewage Purification Works at Jackson Pike also indicated that the treatment process was overloaded and had solids disposal problems. The drying bed operations were analyzed, and it was determined that a depth of six to eight inches "gave a good dry cake without an offensive odor. Utilization of this sludge as a marketable fertilizer is now under investigation with the cooperation of the garbage reduction works."

In 1927, the population's growth outpaced the treatment plant capacity as it was now estimated at 315,000 persons. The state health board ordered the cleanup of Scioto River pollution levels. Once again, the City tapped John H. Gregory to produce construction plans and specifications for a new plant. In 1934, construction on the Jackson Pike Wastewater Treatment Plant, based on the activated sludge process, began at a site adjacent to the 1908 Improved Sewage Works.

CHAPTER SIXTEEN

After the Columbus Experiment and the Players' Fleeting Fame

JERRY O'SHAUGHNESSY

O'Shaughnessy was removed as the city's water superintendent for political reasons in 1908, when Charles A. Bond was elected mayor, and he remained out of office during George S. Marshall's term as mayor. He was reappointed by Mayor George J. Karb on January 1, 1912, and held the position until his death in 1921. He died shortly after his offices were destroyed by a fire that razed the city hall building on State Street. Unfortunately, O'Shaughnessy did not live to see completion of what was then said to be the "best inland city reservoir and dam in the United States." When O'Shaughnessy Dam was completed in 1925, Columbus had a water supply that could service a population of half a million persons, twice the city's size at that time.

JULIAN GRIGGS

After his dismissal in 1908 due to a change in mayoral administration, Griggs did not return to public service and died at the age of seventy-four on December 4, 1922. Two weeks later, on December 18, 1922, the seventeen-year-old Columbus Storage Dam was renamed Julian Griggs Dam.

ALLEN HAZEN

Allen Hazen died while visiting Miles City, Montana. At the time of his death, he was director of the flood control program for the state of New Jersey and many large cities. Allen Hazen resided in Dobbs Ferry, New York and was a month shy of his sixty-first birthday.

JOHN H. GREGORY

Gregory continued working as a consulting engineer until 1919. After serving during World War I as a captain in the Sanitary Corps Medical Department, he became part of the faculty of Johns Hopkins University's School of Engineering. He was the chairman and professor of civil and sanitary engineering and held a similar chair position at the School of Hygiene and Public Health beginning in 1920.

In 1918, Gregory was again employed by the City of Columbus to investigate and report on the water supply for the City. In his reports, Gregory recommended certain reinforcements to the waterworks' distribution system, additions to the water purification and softening works and the construction of a storage dam and reservoir (later named the O'Shaughnessy Dam) on the Scioto River upstream from the Julian Griggs Dam. In the 1930s, Gregory again served as a consultant for the City of Columbus and was project engineer of the new Jackson Pike Wastewater Treatment Plant. This was Gregory's last major project. On January 18, 1937, while packing for a trip to New York, Gregory suffered a heart attack and died.

John H. Gregory bequeathed his entire professional library and papers to the City of Columbus. The impressive collection was housed in a specially designated library in the city hall building on Front Street for a time. As decades passed, the merits of the collection were forgotten. In the 1970s, the library collection was packed up in boxes and stored on the ground floor of a water tower (called a hydro pillar) to make room in city hall. Once the boxes were in storage, they were more or less out of sight and out of mind. Some years later, following a winter power outage that curtailed the heat and resulted in a frozen interior waterline break, a sizable portion of the unprotected boxes containing the priceless records and history of Gregory's life's work were soaked. The mess remained in place for a time until the tank storage area was needed for some other agenda. At that time, city civil service laborers were assigned to heap the damaged material in a dumpster to be conveyed to a landfill. The few boxes that were still intact were given to the Ohio Historical Society on Seventeenth Avenue, adjacent to the state fairgrounds.

CLARENCE HOOVER

In 1921, Clarence Hoover was named resident engineer in charge on construction of the O'Shaughnessy Dam. Shortly thereafter he was named superintendent of the water division, following the death of his predecessor, Jerry O'Shaughnessy. In 1933, he was selected as a member of a group of municipal officials from all parts of the United States who toured Germany for a study of municipal governments there under the auspices of the Karl Schurz Memorial Foundation.

A story Clarence often recalled regarding a visit by a group of Russian visitors to Columbus demonstrates the widespread recognition of the City's water system. Speaking to a local club group, the mayor of Moscow had declared, "We've never heard of Columbus, but we've heard of your waterworks."

Clarence died in 1949 shortly after winning a battle to build a new water storage dam on Big Walnut Creek (Hoover Dam) north of Columbus. Columbus mayor James A. Rhodes issued the following statement: "Mr. Hoover was internationally recognized as one of the outstanding waterworks engineers of the last fifty years. Columbus has lost a conscientious, able and faithful public official, whose farsighted planning for a water supply for the people of this community will remain an enduring monument to his memory. I have lost a very close friend."

CHARLES P. HOOVER

Mr. Hoover went on to co-discover the sterilizing value of the excess lime method of water treatment. As a result of his research, in 1914, he obtained a patent for a simplified process of making sulfate of alumina from bauxite and sulfuric acid. It eliminated the necessity of filtering out the alum of highest purity. Such a process was installed first at the Columbus plant. Another patent, obtained in 1917, related to improvements in the process of making metal hydroxide solutions, such as sodium hydroxide.

Several consulting engineers, not only in Ohio but also throughout the country, retained him to suggest valuable features to incorporate in new municipal water softening plants or for improvements and enlargements proposed for existing plants. Some of the municipal plants on which he collaborated in designing are located in Cedar Rapids, Iowa; Miami, Florida; the Metropolitan Water District of Southern California; and Springfield, Illinois. Charles Hoover died one year after his brother in 1950. In 1955, the Hoover Dam was named in honor of both of the Hoover Brothers.

The next generation of engineers who followed the triumph of the Columbus Experiment was truly committed to expanding on the lessons learned from the project and sharing its benefits with the rest of the world. One in particular stands out as a leader who accepted the challenge of providing potable water in a cost-effective manner.

JAMES MCKEE MONTGOMERY

Montgomery (1896–1969), was born in Columbus, Ohio, and received his bachelor's of science in chemical engineering from Ohio State in 1920 while being mentored by both Clarence B. and Charles P. Hoover. After college, he worked for the Dow Chemical Company and then served as director of public water for the City of Piqua, Ohio, for eight years. After relocating to Columbus, he formed the consulting firm of Hoover and Montgomery with his brother-in-law, Charles P. Hoover. He also invented and received patents on gravimetric and volumetric-chemical feeders, solids-contact clarifiers (a joint patent with William W. Aultman) and a variable throat-venture meter. In 1938, Mr. Montgomery moved to Los Angeles, California, to serve as the resident engineer after the Ohio firm of Hoover and Montgomery was selected to be the design consultant for the Feymouth Memorial Water Softening and Filtration Plant in La Verne. Later, in 1945, he started the firm of James M. Montgomery (JMM).

In 1992, JMM merged with the British engineering firm Watson Hawksley, Ltd., of High Wycombe, England, which was founded in London in the mid-nineteenth century. This created a company with a global scope and one that had similar corporate cultures, honoring individual expertise, as well as encouraging teamwork, innovation and initiative. It also shared a view on the industry's future. In 2001, Montgomery Watson merged with the Harza Engineering Company of Chicago, which was best known for its work in the energy and hydroelectric power development. The name

James M. Montgomery (1896–1969) was a part of the next generation of engineers that followed the Columbus Experiment. He formed a partnership with his brother-in-law, Charles Hoover, starting the Hoover & Montgomery firm, which became the forerunner of James M. Montgomery Consultants and MWH Global. Today, MWH is a renowned global wet-infrastructure engineering firm. *PC.*

was eventually changed to Montgomery Watson Harza and then to MWH Global. The firm is headquartered in Broomfield, Colorado, and has operations in thirty-four countries. As of December 2009, MWH Global had a world staff of over 7,000 employees, including builders, engineers, architects, geologists, operators, project managers, business consultants, scientists, technologists and regulatory experts. In 2008, MWH was listed as number 364 in Forbes's listing of America's Largest Private Companies. Today, it is one of the largest environmental and civil engineering firms operating on an international scale.

CHAPTER SEVENTEEN
The Challenges of the Twenty-first Century

Just as Americans and Central Ohioans have forgotten those associated with the Columbus Experiment and its success, so, too, has the motivational spirit behind the experiment become lost to memory. Although a few were famous for a brief time, no one became wealthy as a result of this endeavor. Most of the technology didn't have a patent, or its originator declined to apply for one. The Columbus Experiment was a giant effort and huge risk on behalf of the general public; it was an attempt to better the lives of everyone, not a venture to acquire wealth or celebrity for a select group of young engineers. Such a project today may have been cancelled because it would have disrupted the habitat of the fauna and flora. For example, darter fish were placed on the endangered species list in the 1980s, and had a dam been proposed at that time, it would have surely been halted.

With so many untimely deaths from waterborne disease, as well as large cities being devastated by fire, the whole concept of urban living and expansion was being severely endangered. This was the motivation behind the Columbus Experiment.

During the latter part of the twentieth century, many new suburban municipalities were established beyond the jurisdiction of the larger central cities to avoid the legacy costs associated with maintaining old infrastructure. This has come with a price because America's water and wastewater systems that were built fifty to one hundred years ago are starting to show serious signs of age deterioration. Hopefully, the general public will begin to view these previous accomplishments as key ingredients in its standard of living

This postcard of Columbus' new water storage was issued in 1911. Postcards like this one served to demonstrate a community's pride in its public works. *CH.*

and quality of life. Although a sizable portion of America's twentieth-century water- and wastewater infrastructure is suffering from age (and in some cases, neglect), this decay presents a great opportunity for future employment in construction and careers in engineering and science. We are now seeing a new generation stepping forward to advance public works to a new level of excellence. It won't be easy, and it will be expensive, but nothing has changed in that regard in the last one hundred years.

In vintage postcard shops and flea markets, one can find postcards of many small community water utilities. These postcards depict early twentieth-century photos of storage dams, pump stations, water towers and fire engines hooked up to hydrants and spraying water high over the county courthouse. These postcards show civic pride and demonstrate that the community pictured was firmly established as a safe haven in which to raise a family. After all, waterborne disease bacteria are always with us, and building fires will occur. But a community that is equipped with a supply of water and a means to treat and pump it through a network of pipes will be prepared for the challenge of nature.

The Hinds Family Connection to the Columbus Experiment

During the three years between the death of President William F. McKinley and the premature death of Senator Marcus Hanna from typhoid fever, the United States took steps to acquire and complete the Panama Canal project initiated by the French twenty years earlier. The new president, Theodore Roosevelt, and the late Senator Marcus Hanna were two of the prime promoters of this venture. President Roosevelt placed Ohioan William Howard Taft in charge of the Panama Canal project, and in 1904, Taft recommended recruiting English-speaking laborers from Barbados and other Caribbean islands to work on the canal.

Two of the fifty thousand recruits were named John and Louise Hinds, who were my paternal grandparents. Family history tells me that my paternal grandparents were from Barbados. They settled in the Canal Zone community of Colon; had seven children, all of whom were girls; and in 1926, my father, the late Dr. Conrade C. Hinds Sr. was born. As a teenager, he worked as a carpenter to help build the first high school in Colon, Panama. He graduated at age twenty-one and received a track and field athletic scholarship to Fisk University in Nashville, Tennessee. After graduating with a degree in solid state physics, he moved his young family to Wilberforce, Ohio, where he began teaching college-level physics. At the age of thirty-seven, he was appointed chairman of the physics department at Southern University in Baton Rouge, Louisiana. In addition, he worked with other physicists at the NASA research center in Huntsville, Alabama, on the development of the Saturn V rocket, which took the first astronauts to the moon.

Above: Photograph of a display showing Charles P. Hoover working in his water-testing laboratory. The display is part of a water education program and plant tour presentation that began in 1995 at the historic Dublin Road Water Plant, located at 940 Dublin Road, Columbus, Ohio. *CH.*

Left: A working scale replica of the Holly Triple-Expansion Engine and Pump was custom built by precision machinist William Clark in 1995. It is on public display at the Dublin Road Water Plant in Columbus, Ohio. *CH.*

After my father received his doctorate in science education from Ball State University in 1971, I began college at Ball State and majored in architecture and industrial technology. After college, I returned to Ohio and soon found myself working for John Circle, the newly elected engineer for Franklin County. I met Mr. Circle and a number of other elected County officials while attending a Lincoln-McKinley Dinner fundraiser. Three years later, the Franklin County treasurer, Dana Rinehart, was elected mayor of Columbus, and I was appointed to begin work at the Columbus Department of Public Utilities, Division of Water.

As an architect and historian, I was very curious about water treatment facilities and their history, both past and present. In honoring the forward thinking of Senator Marcus Hanna 100 years earlier, I made use of the forgotten and historic wealth of knowledge found in over 120 years of overlooked reports, charts and photographs about the community's forgotten heritage surrounding the 1908 Columbus Experiment.

Headlines 1903-1908

The Columbus Experiment was a century ago and for many today it is difficult to see any connection to that time or era. But let's not forget that who we are in many ways was determined by the events and people of previous times. The baby boomers, their parents and grandparents and beyond were born and raised with a quality of life closely associated with the success of the Columbus Experiment. These generations were not concerned with typhoid and cholera epidemics. Fires in most urban and suburban areas were generally confined to a single building or facility without threatening to destroy the entire community. The following is a brief overview of events, births and a few deaths that occurred during the key years of the Columbus Experiment (1903–1908) that may have touched or had a small connection to our lives.

1903 EVENTS

FEBRUARY 15—Morris and Rose Michtom introduce the first Teddy Bear in America. Morris Michtom (1870–1938) was a Russian Jewish immigrant, who with his wife, Rose, invented the Teddy Bear. Michtom arrived in New York in 1887 and sold candy in his shop at 404 Tompkins Avenue in Bedford-Stuyvesant Brooklyn by day and made stuffed animals with his wife at night. The Teddy Bear was a response to a cartoon by Clifford K. Berryman depicting President Theodore Roosevelt showing compassion for a bear at the end of an unsuccessful hunting trip in Mississippi in

1902. After the creation of the bear in 1902, the sale of the bears was so brisk that Michtom created the Ideal Novelty and Toy Company.

MARCH 14—The Hay-Herran Treaty, which granted the United States the right to build the Panama Canal, is ratified by the United States Senate. The Colombian Senate later rejected the treaty.

JUNE 16—Henry Ford founds and incorporates the Ford Motor Company in Dearborn, Michigan.

NOVEMBER 13—The United States formally recognizes the independence of Panama.

NOVEMBER 18—The Hay-Bunau-Varilla Treaty is signed by the United States and Panama, giving the U.S. exclusive rights over the Panama Canal Zone.

DECEMBER 17—Orville Wright flies an aircraft with a petrol engine at Kitty Hawk, North Carolina in the first documented, successful, controlled, powered, heavier-than-air flight.

DECEMBER 30—A fire at the Iroquois Theatre in Chicago kills 600; The first box of Crayola crayons was made and sold for 5 cents. It contained eight colors: brown, red, orange, yellow, green, blue, violet and black.

BIRTHS

APRIL 19—Eliot Ness, American treasury agent (d. 1957)

MAY 2—Benjamin Spock, American pediatrician (d. 1998)

MAY 3—Bing Crosby, American singer and actor (d. 1977)

MAY 29—Bob Hope, English-born American comedian and actor (d. 2003)

JUNE 19—Lou Gehrig, American baseball player (d. 1941)

AUGUST 31—Arthur Godfrey, American radio and television host (d. 1983)

SEPTEMBER 21—Preston Tucker, automobile designer (d. 1956)

OCTOBER 22—Three Stooges actor Jerome "Curly Howard" Horwitz (d. 1952)

DECEMBER 28—Earl Hines, American jazz pianist (d. 1983)

DEATHS

MARCH 16—Roy Bean, American pioneer (b. 1825)

AUGUST 1—Calamity Jane, American frontierswoman (b. 1852)

1904 EVENTS

JANUARY 12—Henry Ford sets a new automobile land speed record of 91.37 miles per hour.

FEBRUARY 7—The Great Baltimore Fire in Baltimore, Maryland, destroys over 1,500 buildings in 30 hours.

FEBRUARY 8—A Japanese surprise attack on Port Arthur (Lushun) starts the Russo-Japanese War. Called "the first great war of the twentieth century," the Russo-Japanese War grew out of rival imperial ambitions of the Russian Empire and Japanese Empire over Manchuria and Korea.

FEBRUARY 23—The United States pays $10 million to gain control of the Panama Canal Zone. An engineering study favored a canal using a lock system to raise and lower ships from a large reservoir eighty-five feet above sea level and was recommended to President Theodore Roosevelt by chief engineer John Frank Stevens and approved by the president. The 115-foot-high Gatun Dam would create both the largest dam and the largest man-made lake.

APRIL 30—The Louisiana Purchase Exposition World's Fair opens in St. Louis, Missouri (closes December 1).

MAY 4—The United States, after purchasing the French equipment and excavations which included the Panama Railroad for $40 million, begins work on the Panama Canal.

OCTOBER 27—The first underground line of the New York City Subway opens.

NOVEMBER 24—The first successful caterpillar track is made.

DECEMBER 31—The first New Year's Eve celebration is held in Times Square in New York.

BIRTHS

JANUARY 10—Ray Bolger, actor, singer and dancer (*The Wizard of Oz*) (d. 1987)

JANUARY 18—Cary Grant, actor (d. 1986)

FEBRUARY 16—James Baskett, actor, known for his portrayal of Uncle Remus in Disney's *Song of the South* (d. 1948)

FEBRUARY 29—Jimmy Dorsey, American bandleader (d. 1957)

MARCH 1—Glenn Miller, American bandleader (d. 1944)

MARCH 2—Dr. Seuss, American children's author (d. 1991)

APRIL 14—Sir John Gielgud, English actor (d. 2000)

APRIL 18—Dewey "Pigmeat" Marcusham, African American entertainer (d. 1981)

APRIL 22—Robert Oppenheimer, American physicist (d. 1967)

MAY 11—Salvador Dalí, Spanish artist (d. 1989)

MAY 21—Fats Waller, American pianist and comedian (d. 1943)

JUNE 2—Johnny Weissmuller, American swimmer and actor, known for his portrayal of Tarzan (d. 1984)

JUNE 26—Peter Lorre, Hungarian-born film actor (d. 1964)

AUGUST 21—Count Basie, musician and bandleader (d. 1984)

DEATHS

FEBRUARY 15—Marcus Hanna, United States senator (b. 1837)

1905 EVENTS

FEBRUARY 23—The Rotary International is founded.

MARCH 4—U.S. president Theodore Roosevelt begins a full term.

MAY 15—One hundred and ten acres of what is present-day downtown Las Vegas, Nevada, is auctioned off and the city founded.

OCTOBER 5—The Wright Brothers' third airplane (Wright Flyer III) stays in the air for thirty-nine minutes with Wilbur piloting, the first airplane flight lasting over half an hour.

OCTOBER 16—The Russian army opens fire on a meeting at a street market in Tallinn, killing ninety-four people and injuring over two hundred, launching the Russian Revolution of 1905.

Also this year, Mark Twain novels *The Adventures of Huckleberry Finn* and *The Adventures of Tom Sawyer* are banned from the Brooklyn Public Library for setting a "bad example." Alfred Einhorn introduces novocaine.

BIRTHS

MAY 16—Henry Fonda, actor (*The Grapes of Wrath*) (d. 1982)

JULY 29—Dag Hammarskjöld, secretary general of the Swedish United Nations (d. 1961)

AUGUST 2—Myrna Loy, American actress (d. 1993)

AUGUST 21—Friz Freleng, "Looney Tunes" director (d. 1995)

NOVEMBER 15—Mantovani, Italian-born conductor and arranger (d. 1980)

DECEMBER 24—Howard Hughes, multimillionaire, aviation pioneer and film mogul (d. 1976)

DEATHS

FEBRUARY 15—Lew Wallace, American writer who authored *Ben-Hur: A Tale of the Christ* (b. 1827)

MARCH 24—Jules Verne, French science fiction author who wrote *Twenty Thousand Leagues Under the Sea* (b. 1828)

1906 EVENTS

APRIL 18—San Francisco earthquake (estimated magnitude 7.8) on the San Andreas Fault destroys much of San Francisco, California, killing at least 3,000 and leaving 225,000–300,000 homeless. It caused an estimated $350 million in damages.

JUNE 7—The world's largest ship, the RMS *Lusitania*, is launched in Glasgow.

AUGUST 22—The first Victor Victrola, a phonographic record player, is manufactured.

SEPTEMBER 11—Mahatma Gandhi coins the term Satyagraha to characterize the non-violence movement in South Africa.

SEPTEMBER 18—A typhoon and tsunami kill an estimated ten thousand people in Hong Kong.

NOVEMBER 3—SOS becomes an international distress signal; The Bacillus Calmette-Guérin (BCG) immunization for tuberculosis is first developed.

BIRTHS

FEBRUARY 5—John Carradine, actor (d. 1988)

FEBRUARY 10—Lon Chaney, Jr., actor (d. 1973); Lou Costello, actor (d. 1959)

APRIL 22—Eddie Albert, actor (d. 2005)

MAY 3—Mary Astor, actress and writer (d. 1987)

JUNE 22—Anne Morrow Lindbergh, American author and aviator (d. 2001)

July 1—Estée Lauder, cosmetics entrepreneur (d. 2004)

JULY 7—Satchel Paige, baseball player (d. 1982)

NOVEMBER 15—Curtis LeMay, U.S. Air Force general from Columbus, Ohio (d. 1990)

DECEMBER 5—Otto Preminger, Austrian-born American film director (d. 1986)

DECEMBER 9—Grace Hopper, computer scientist and naval officer (d. 1992)

DECEMBER 19—Leonid Brezhnev, Soviet leader (d. 1982)
DECEMBER 27—Oscar Levant, pianist, composer, author and actor (d. 1972)

DEATHS

FEBRUARY 27—Samuel Pierpont Langley, astronomer, physicist and aeronautics pioneer (b. 1834)
OCTOBER 22—Paul Cézanne, French painter (b. 1839)

1907 EVENTS

JANUARY 6—The first Montessori school and daycare center for working class children opens in Rome.
AUGUST 1–August 9—Robert Baden-Powell leads the first Scout camp on Brownsea Island, England.
OCTOBER 17—Guglielmo Marconi initiates commercial transatlantic radio communications between his high power long wave wireless telegraphy stations in Clifden, Ireland, and Glace Bay, Nova Scotia.
DECEMBER 6—Monongah Mining Disaster: A coal mine explosion kills 362 workers in Monongah, West Virginia.
DECEMBER 19—An explosion in a coal mine in Jacobs Creek, Pennsylvania, kills 239.

BIRTHS

February 15—Cesar Romero, actor (d. 1994)
February 17—Buster Crabbe, swimmer and actor (d. 1983)
February 22—Sheldon Leonard, actor, director and producer (d. 1997); Robert Young, actor (d. 1998)
May 12—Katharine Hepburn, actress (d. 2003)
May 22—Lord Laurence Olivier, English stage and screen actor and director (d. 1989)
May 26—John Wayne, actor (d. 1979)
September 29—Gene Autry, actor, singer and businessman (d. 1998)
November 16—Burgess Meredith, actor (d. 1997)
November 23—Run Run Shaw, Hong Kong media mogul
December 15—Oscar Niemeyer, Brazilian architect
December 23—James Roosevelt, American businessman and politician (d. 1991)

Deaths

May 26—Ida Saxton McKinley, American first lady (b. 1847)

1908 Events

January 12—A long-distance radio message is sent from the Eiffel Tower for the first time.
January 13—A fire at the Rhoads Opera House in Boyertown, Pennsylvania, kills 170.
January 24—Robert Baden-Powell begins the Boy Scout movement.
March 4—The Collinwood School Fire, near Cleveland, Ohio, kills 174.
August 8—Wilbur Wright flies in France for the first time, demonstrating true controlled powered flight.
August 17—Emile Cohl makes the first fully animated film, *Fantasmagorie*.
September 17—Thomas Selfridge becomes the first person to die in an airplane crash at Fort Myer, Virginia; The pilot, Orville Wright, is severely injured in the crash but recovers.
September 27—Henry Ford produces his first Model T automobile.

Births

January 15—Edward Teller, Hungarian-born physicist (d. 2003)
February 1—George Pal, Hungarian-born animator (d. 1980)
February 22—John Mills, English actor (d. 2005)
March 5—Rex Harrison, English actor (d. 1990)
March 22—Louis L'Amour, American author (d. 1988)
April 1—Abraham Maslow, American psychologist (d. 1970)
April 2—Buddy Ebsen, actor (*Beverly Hillbillies*) and dancer (d. 2003)
April 5—Bette Davis, actress (d. 1989)
April 20—Lionel Hampton, African American musician and bandleader (d. 2002)
April 28—Oskar Schindler, Austro-Hungarian (Sudeten German) industrialist (d. 1974)
April 30—Eve Arden, actress (d. 1990)
May 20—James Stewart, actor (d. 1997)
May 23—Max Abramovitz, architect (d. 2004)
May 28—Ian Fleming, James Bond author (d. 1964); Mel Blanc, voice actor (d. 1989)

MAY 31—Don Ameche, actor (d. 1993)

JULY 12—Milton Berle, actor, comedian (d. 2002); Lyndon Johnson, U.S. president (d. 1973); Fred MacMurray, actor (d. 1991)

OCTOBER 15—John Kenneth Galbraith, Canadian economist (d. 2006)

NOVEMBER 20—Alistair Cooke, English-born journalist (d. 2004)

DECEMBER 31—Simon Wiesenthal, Austrian Nazi-hunter (d. 2005)

DEATHS

JUNE 24—Grover Cleveland, twenty-second and twenty-fourth president of the United States (b. 1837)

NOVEMBER 7—Butch Cassidy, American outlaw (b. 1866)

SOME GENERAL QUOTES IN THE SPIRIT OF OHIO AND THE COLUMBUS EXPERIMENT

It is possible to fly without motors, but not without knowledge and skill.
—Wilbur Wright

Men become wise just as they become rich, more by what they save than by what they receive.
—Wilbur Wright

Don't fight forces, use them.
—R. Buckminster Fuller

There will always be a frontier where there is an open mind.
—Charles F. Kettering

America's rapid growth made it a strong country, but its slow maturity is hastening its decline.
—Conrade C. Hinds

Bibliography

NEWSPAPERS

Columbus Citizen Journal
Columbus Dispatch
Columbus Evening Dispatch

BOOKS AND ARTICLES

Asimov, Isaac, Asimov's Biographical Encyclopedia of Science and Technology. 2nd ed. New York: Doubleday, 1982.

Bales, Richard F. *Did the Cow Do It? A New Look at the Cause of the Great Chicago Fire.* Springfield: Illinois State Historical Society, 1997.

Bourdain, Anthony. *Typhoid Mary: An Urban Historical.* New York: Bloomsbury, 2001.

Brandt, Nat. *Chicago Death Trap: The Iroquois Theatre Fire of 1903.* Carbondale: Southern Illinois University Press, 2003.

Brookhart, J. Douglas, and Alvin D. Wansing. *History of Ohio's Water Systems.* Columbus: Ohio Section American Water Works Association, 2010.

Byrne, Joseph P., *Encyclopedia of Pestilence, Pandemics, and Plagues.* Westport, CT: Greenwood Publishing Group, 2008.

City of Columbus, Ohio, Department of Public Service. Annual Reports for the years 1889, 1890, 1903, 1904, 1905, 1906, 1907, 1908, 1910.

Civil War Society. *Encyclopedia of the Civil War.* New York: Random House Publishing, 1997.

Clarke, Robert. *Ellen Swallow: The Women Who Founded Ecology.* Chicago, IL: Follett Publishing, 1973.

"Collinwood School Fire 1908." *The Encyclopedia of Cleveland History.* Bloomington: Indiana University Press, 1987.

Fredrickson, Madelynn P. *The Life and Times of Birdsill Holly.* Rome, GA: Blue Spruce Publishing, 1996.

Gould, Lewis L. *The Presidency of William McKinley.* Lawrence: University Press of Kansas, 1980.

Gradmann, Christoph. *Laboratory Disease: Robert Koch's Medical Bacteriology.* Baltimore, MD: Johns Hopkins University Press, 2009.

Gregory, John H. "The Improved Water and Sewage Works of Columbus, Ohio." *Transactions of the American Society of Civil Engineers* 67, no. 1146 (1910).

Hanninen, O., M. Farago and E. Monos. "Ignaz Philipp Semmelweis: The Prophet of Bacteriology." *Infect Control* (1983): 367–70.

Hatch, Anthony P. *Tinder Box: The Iroquois Theatre Disaster, 1903.* Chicago: Academy Chicago Publishers, 2003.

Hays, J.N. *Epidemics and Pandemics: Their Impacts on Human History.* Santa Barbara, CA: ABC-CLIO, 2005.

Hill, Libby. *The Chicago River: A Natural and Unnatural History.* Chicago: Lake Claremont Press, 2000.

Horner, William T. *Ohio's Kingmaker: Marcus Hanna, Man and Myth.* Athens: Ohio University Press, 2010.

Hutcheson, Edwin. *Floods of Johnstown: 1889, 1936, 1977.* Johnstown, PA: Cambria County Tourist Council, 1989.

Johnson, George A. *Report on Sewage Purification.* Columbus, OH: City of Columbus, 1905.

Jones, Stanley L. *The Presidential Election of 1896.* Madison: University of Wisconsin Press, 1964.

Lamont, Ann. "Joseph Lister: Father of Modern Surgery." *Creation Magazine* (March 1992): 48–51.

Lawson, Andrew C. *The California Earthquake of April 18, 1906: Report of the State Earthquake Investigation Commission.* Washington, D.C., Carnegie Institution of Washington Publication 87, 1908.

Leech, Margaret. *In the Days of McKinley.* New York: Harper and Brothers, 1959.

McCullough, David. *The Johnstown Flood*. 1968. Reprint. New York: Simon & Schuster, 1987.

———. *The Path Between the Seas: The Creation of the Panama Canal, 1870–1914*. New York: Touchstone, 1997.

McElroy, Richard L. *William McKinley and Our America*. Canton, OH: Stark County Historical Society, 1996.

Miller, Scott. *The President and the Assassin*. New York: Random House, 2011.

Nuland, Sherwin B. *Doctors: The Biography of Medicine*. New York: Knopf, 1998. Olson, Sherry H. *Baltimore: The Building of an American City*. Baltimore, MD: Johns Hopkins University Press, 1997.

Seck, Momar and David Evans. "Major U.S. Cities Using National Standard Fire Hydrants, One Century after the Great Baltimore Fire." *National Institute of Standards and Technology*. (August 2004): 7–9

Slattery, Gertrude Quinn. *Johnstown Flood*. Wilkes-Barre, PA: Wilkes-Barre Publishing, 1936.

Williams, David J. *The History of Burgess & Niple, 1912–1992*. Cleveland, OH: Emerson Press, 1992.

About the Author

Conrade C. Hinds is a registered architect in Ohio and New York and a retired project manager for the City of Columbus Division of Water. Originally from Nashville, Tennessee, Hinds has spent the last thirty-five years living in Central Ohio and worked as an adjunct faculty member in the engineering technology department at Columbus State Community College for twenty-four years. He is a master at yodeling, a storyteller and a historian who often incorporates the use of puppets and marionettes in his presentations. Mr. Hinds also serves on the board of the Columbus Landmarks Foundation and is a member of the Ohio Memorial Chapter of the Tuskegee Airmen. He is married to Dr. Janet L. Hinds, and they have four children and two grandchildren.

Visit us at
www.historypress.net